Convair 880 & 990

By Jon Proctor

This book is dedicated to those who envisioned, built, maintained, and flew the Convair 880 & 990.

Published by

WORLD TRANSPORT PRESS, INC.

P.O. Box 521238
Miami, Fla. 33152-1238
Tel. +1 (305) 477-7163
Fax +1 (305) 599-1995

CREDITS

PHOTOGRAPHS:
FRONT COVER
Top: Thomas Livesey Collection.
Bottom: Jay Miller

TITLE PAGE
© LARRY PULLEN

BACK COVER
General Dynamics photos courtesy of the San Diego Aerospace Museum.

COVER DESIGN AND SERIES LOGO
RANDY WILHELM, ART DIRECTOR
KEOKEE COMPANY
SANDPOINT, IDAHO

Unless otherwise indicated, non-captioned photos are courtesy of General Dynamics Corporation

Table of Contents

FOREWORD

It is difficult to find books written about airplanes perceived as commercial flops. Too bad, because sometimes the stories of such failures are as dramatic and fascinating as those of more successful aircraft.

In the well-researched tale you are about to read, Jon Proctor has accomplished just such a goal. The Convair 880 and 990 jetliners were classic examples of "might-have-been" transports, financial flops but — in so many ways — technological triumphs that deserved better fates, and certainly deserving to have their stories told.

The 880 in particular was an underrated airliner of enormous strength, victimized more by marketing difficulties (such as its narrow, three-and-two seating configuration) than design deficiencies. Pilots loved it but flight attendants preferred Boeing and Douglas cabins.

Nevertheless, the 880 and the somewhat over-hyped 990 made their own contributions to the Jet Age, and in this account Jon Proctor has made an important contribution to aviation history.

Robert J. Serling

INTRODUCTION

Coming from an airline family, I was attracted to the Convair jets when we moved from Chicago to the San Diego area in 1957. By then, the 880 program was well under way at the company's Lindbergh Field headquarters, followed shortly by the General Dynamics announcement which formally launched the Model 600, later known as the 990.

The new jetliner programs received wide media coverage, and I had several high school classmates whose parents worked either for Convair or one of the local support companies. Being an airliner buff, I spent many hours around Lindbergh Field, and was able to catch an occasional glimpse of these sleek jetliners as they completed flight testing prior to customer delivery. This experience helped me develop a keen interest in Convair's jets which remained even after I left the area in 1963.

A year later, Trans World Airlines was hiring ticket agents at Los Angeles, and I was fortunate enough to join the carrier operating the world's largest 880 fleet. As the son of a retired American Airlines pilot, I had also been exposed to the largest 990 operator. Upon joining the American Aviation Historical Society, it seemed to me that the subject of Convair's jets would make a good research project. My efforts appeared in that organization's Fall and Winter 1976 journals, split into two parts.

Twenty years later, all these airplanes have disappeared from the skies, and it is appropriate to take another look at a story which stirs vivid memories for aviation aficionados. Many considered the 880 to be the thoroughbred of America's early jetliners. Sitting a little closer to the ground than its competitors, and with sleek lines, it even *looked* fast. Then came the 990, with its unique wing-mounted speed pods.

Perhaps their relatively brief life spans helped to assure the Convair jets' place in airline folklore. For whatever reason, very few people have a bad word to say about either airplane. Indeed, just the mention of one seems to bring out an emotional attachment from those who remember them, especially pilots, who usually want to talk at great length about the 880 and 990. During conversations numerous war stories were coupled with suggestions that I talk to others who would also regale me with their own "Convairisms."

From these countless recollections and many hours of research comes a book which I hope will entertain as it informs. If there seems to be holes in the story, remember that it began more than 40 years ago. Tracking down certain details led to dead ends, and speculation — for the most part — has been left out. Any corrections or information on topics not mentioned would be appreciated.

The story of Convair's finest is, at times, painful to read. But mistakes and lost opportunities should not overshadow their substantial contribution of civil aviation during the early years of turbojet operations.

PART I

THE CONVAIR 880

CHAPTER ONE: DEVELOPMENT

The Boeing 707 and Douglas DC-8 preceded Convair's 880 into service by 19 months; the 990 followed two years later. Conceived as the world's fastest transports, the Convair jets suffered from reduced capacity and high operating costs which brought about their early demise. Except for a single 990, the few remaining examples rest in museums or storage yards, and have not flown commercially for many years.

These unique models were developed with many features considered well-advanced for their time. Built like tanks, each provided reliable service for their owners and were preferred by customers and air crews alike.

But this is not a success story. Parent company General Dynamics (GD) lost $425 million building 102 airplanes.

Convair's Genealogy

Convair's corporate history began in 1908, when former physics professor Edson F. Gallaudet organized the Gallaudet Aircraft Corporation. In 1923, Gallaudet merged with the Dayton-Wright Airplane Company to form Consolidated Aircraft Corporation, a successful builder of land- and seaplanes. Acquiring other companies as it grew, Consolidated immigrated from Buffalo, New York to San Diego, California in 1935. Employment exceeded 3,000 by 1940, and ballooned to 33,000 by the time America entered World War II.

Vultee Aircraft, Inc. grew out of two companies, formed by aviation pioneers Eddie Stinson and Jerry Vultee. It was incorporated in 1939 as a subsidiary of the Aviation Corporation and contributed heavily to the war effort.

In 1943, the companies joined to form Consolidated Vultee Corporation. The fourth largest U.S. industrial military contractor, it became the nation's most prolific aircraft builder, producing more than 30,000 planes during World War II.

As hostilities ended, the company began shedding military capacity, but continued to produce bomber and fighter types at its San Diego and Fort Worth, Texas plants, including the B-36, B-58, F-102, and F-106.

At the same time, attention was directed toward the commercial airliner market. A passenger transport variant of the B-24 Liberator bomber, the C-87, had seen military use during the war, but its limited seating capacity precluded later airline sales. The slightly larger Model 101, also flown by the armed forces, evolved into the Model 39 Liberator Liner, designed to carry up to 48 passengers. Tested briefly in a cargo role by American Airlines, it did not attract orders. Too many military surplus aircraft, such as the C-54 and, to a lesser degree, the C-69, were readily available.

The Convair-Liner

Thousands of C-47s, military versions of the venerable DC-3, were also flooding the market. However the airlines wanted a newer twin-engine short- to medium-range design, incorporating cabin pressurization and increased speed, to serve the rapid growth in post-war passenger traffic.

Right:
The Convair 240
(General Dynamics)

Below: *San Diego's Lindbergh Field, circa 1958, with Convair's plant visible in the upper left.*
(General Dynamics)

Consolidated Vultee was now recognized as "Convair" by condensing Con(solidated)-V(ultee)-Air, although the division name would not become official until General Dynamics Corporation (GD) completed its acquisition of the operation in 1954. From this identity came Convair-Liner, a name given to the company's proposed DC-3 replacement.

Produced at San Diego, the prototype Model 110 first flew on July 8, 1946. From this 30-seat design, the production Model 240 was developed, gaining its name from the *two*-engine, *forty*-passenger arrangement. The tricycle landing gear configuration and pressurized cabin alone were a marked improvement over the DC-3 design, further enhanced by a substantial increase in cruising speed.

Convair-Liner production was assured by a 100-plane order (later reduced to 75), from American Airlines, which began 240 operations on June 1, 1948. Featuring integral boarding stairs and carry-on luggage racks, the sturdy new 240s were welcomed to the fleets of 13 airlines plus a few corporate customers. Second-hand examples eventually migrated to many other carriers worldwide. A total of 176 civil 240s was built, plus 390 military T-29 and C-131A versions sold to the United States Air Force.

Initially known as the 240A, Convair's improved Model 340 was stretched 4.5 feet, allowing four additional passenger seats for a capacity of 44. A larger wing provided the performance improvements necessary to attract United Air Lines, which ordered 30 examples (and eventually took 55). UAL operated the first Convair 340 service on November 16, 1952. Civil production totaled 209, with an additional 102 going to the U.S. Navy and Air Force.

Minor modifications to the 340 design brought about the Convair 440 Metropolitan which offered a slightly higher gross weight, more quiet cabin and optional radar installation. Continental Airlines introduced the type, on March 8, 1956. Convair offered modification kits which brought 340 models up to near-440 standards; about 100 were so converted.

With the 199 Model 440s, including military variants, Convair-Liner production reached 1,076

units including the prototype 110. The last examples came off the Lindbergh Field assembly line in early 1958, although some were not sold until 1960.

Three different turboprop-engine-conversion programs increased the service lives of many examples, some of which are still in service today, although principally in the role of cargo transports. One of the options resulted in actual airframe production under license, by Canadair, Ltd. at Montréal, Canada, where 10 examples were produced. Another modification, also undertaken by a Canadian firm, brought about the stretched Convair 5800 freighter, which may eventually further extend the useful life of these sturdy aircraft.

Birth of a Jetliner

In 1953 Convair was already looking for a new design to eventually replace its highly successful twin-engine series.

Early that year, billionaire Howard Hughes became interested in the possibility of converting Convair's experimental eight-engine YB-60 jet bomber into a commercial transport, for use by Trans World Airlines, in which he held controlling stock. A feasibility study quickly ruled out pursuing the idea further, and the airplane never went into production. However, these talks marked the beginning of a relationship between Hughes and Convair that eventually would produce the 880.

The eccentric Mr. Hughes was no stranger to civil aviation. After gaining control of TWA in 1938, he participated in the design of virtually all aircraft acquired for the airline. This practice started with the Lockheed Constellation, with which he became intimately involved, from its point of conception until the final 1649A model arrived in 1957. He would buy airplanes through his wholly-owned Hughes Tool Company (Toolco), lease them to TWA and deduct the depreciation costs from Toolco's gross earnings, substantially reducing corporate income taxes.

Convair officials became disenchanted with Hughes three years before the YB-60 discussions, when he ordered from competitor Glenn L. Martin Company, after negotiating for Convair 240s. Although Convair apparently bungled the deal, secretive conferences called by Mr. Hughes, usually in the middle of the night, did little to cement a relationship with the manufacturer.

This strange practice continued in July 1953, when a meeting was held in a guarded, otherwise empty ballroom at a Southern California hotel. Hughes and TWA's head of engineering, Robert Rummel, along with Convair vice-president Jack Zevely and his chief engineer, Ralph Bayless, reviewed Convair's specifications for a proposed 68-passenger jet transport. Although interested, Hughes considered it insufficient in terms of size and range for TWA's purposes, and requested a bigger, long-haul design.

Discussions with Convair, code-named "Project Southern Comfort," continued through 1954 and into 1955 at locations all over the United States. Many proposed designs were considered, including pure-jet, turboprop and hybrid configurations, powered by a host of different engine

Early Skylark 600 representation in Delta colors.
(General Dynamics)

types. Some unconventional jet-powered domestic versions were beefed up with extra turboprop engines to attain trans-Atlantic range. According to Bob Rummel, Hughes attended several of the meetings and reviewed various proposals, but did not take part in the actual design process.

Early in 1955, Convair unveiled a four-engine jet transport design, capable of carrying 123 passengers (in six-abreast all-coach seating) over domestic routes, and powered by Pratt & Whitney

JT-3 engines. A bigger overseas version, accommodating an additional 24 seats, would utilize uprated JT-4 power plants. Both had fuselage diameters greater than Boeing or Douglas. The Model 18 carried a proposed July 1958 certification date, which would allow it to enter service ahead of the competition.

To assure a large order, Convair offered to sell the first 30 ships to Hughes. Giving so many initial delivery positions to one company was unheard of, and would eliminate early acquisitions by other prospective customers. To grant such a favor to the unorthodox Howard Hughes was even more incredible. Needless to say, he was very interested in pursuing the deal.

But when Boeing and Douglas both announced plans to produce similar passenger jets, Convair managers realized the airline market could not support three types with essentially the same capabilities, and shelved the Model 18 project; a formal announcement came on July 28, 1955. Shortly thereafter, Convair offered two new options, the Models 19 and 20, representing much heavier, longer-range designs, but neither was taken seriously.

Meanwhile, Howard Hughes considered both the de Havilland Comet IV and Bristol Britannia, before finally ordering 707s, several months after both American and Pan Am had made large commitments for the Boeings. Hughes even considered having his Hughes Aircraft division produce jetliners for TWA, but abandoned the plan.

Convair, still intent on producing a commercial jetliner, proposed the Model 22 "Skylark 600" to Hughes in March 1956. Essentially a down-sized Model 18, it would carry 80 passengers over segments from medium-range up to and including transcontinental non-stops, at 600 mph cruising speeds, hence the 600 designation.

Again, Toolco was offered generous delivery rights. This time it was for the first 40 airplanes, a number dictated by General Dynamics' board of directors as the minimum required for a project launch. It represented 60 per cent of the 68 ships considered necessary to break even financially.

It has been said that for Convair to pursue the medium- rather than short-range market was a mistake. The Skylark's range, just slightly less than Boeing's domestic 707 model, made it a medium- to long-range airplane. However, the U.S. local service carriers were not in a financial position to purchase expensive new jet equipment. Acquisitions were limited to second-hand aircraft and, later, Fairchild F-27s. Convair further argued that a suitable engine for a 50- to 100-seat airplane was not available.

The Golden Arrow

Skylark presentations were made to several interested airlines, but concentrated on Howard Hughes, and Convair custom-designed the proposal to attract an order for TWA.

Original plans utilized Pratt & Whitney's J-57 engine for the new airplane, but in early 1956 a switch was made to the General Electric J-79 when it was learned that the power plant was soon be released by the military for commercial use. The civilian CJ-805 design offered a better power-to-weight ratio and lower fuel consumption than the JT3 commercial version of the J-57. The GE civilian version, without an afterburner, would have a fixed-area nozzle installed to replace the variable arrangement.

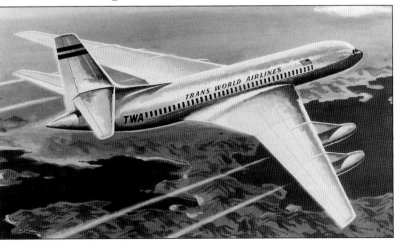

An original Golden Arrow publicity photo. (General Dynamics)

Pratt & Whitney pressured TWA and Convair to adopt its new "bypass" model, still in the development stage. Although heavier than the JT3, it would produce greater thrust. The proposal was rejected, apparently by both parties, because it would require a wing re-design, and delay initial aircraft deliveries.

The Skylark's wings, thinner than the Boeing and Douglas designs to enhance speed, would sweep back at a 35 degree angle, yet its span of 118 feet, 4 inches provided sufficient lift to allow operation from 5,000 foot runways. However, such stringent speed and range requirements aerodynamically restricted the fuselage to a width sufficient for no more than five-abreast seating in coach. This, Convair reasoned, would be adequate for its target markets. Meanwhile, Boeing and Douglas had acquiesced to customers and, with lower design speeds, were able to widen the 707 and DC-8 layouts to accommodate six-across arrangements.

Revenue performance figures for the Skylark were predicated on all-first-class layouts, 615 mph cruise speeds, 25 minute ground stops and high aircraft utilization. Using this reasoning, the airplane could break even on a medium-haul flight with only 30 percent of the seats filled.

Again, Howard Hughes was enthusiastic and told Convair "I'm your first customer," but he only wanted 30 airplanes. In order to meet minimum program launch requirements, Delta Air Lines was allowed to acquire 10 of the first batch of 40 ships, although Toolco would retain the right to designate Delta's delivery positions.

Preliminary contracts were signed June 7, 1956, between Toolco, Delta, General Electric and Convair. Press releases announced the official launch of the "Golden Arrow," replacing the Skylark name of only nine months. Originally intended for the Model 18 proposal and heavily promoted by Howard Hughes, the new name was intended to create an image of speed

and luxury. With it came plans to incorporate a "shimmering gold" exterior metal that would make the airplane stand out from "conventionally colored transports."

To secure Toolco's order, Hughes had to put down just $15 million, or ten percent of the total, with no further payments until the first airplane was delivered three years later.

The 880 Emerges

By the time Delta and TWA reached formal agreements with Convair (on September 10, 1956), the Skylark 600 designation was changed to "880," which equaled the plane's design speed of 600 mph in feet per second. According to an unnamed airline executive, the true origin came from the 88-seat capacity, plus a zero, added because, "They didn't want it to sound like a piano." However, it appears that the change came about prior to the capacity increase, which gives credence to the feet per second story.

The Golden Arrow plan was also dropped. Several airlines were already marketing golden themes, including Eastern and Air France. Continental strenuously objected, claiming to have already advertised plans for its own Golden Arrow flights.

Convair engineers knew that it was impossible to produce exterior gold-colored skin with a con-

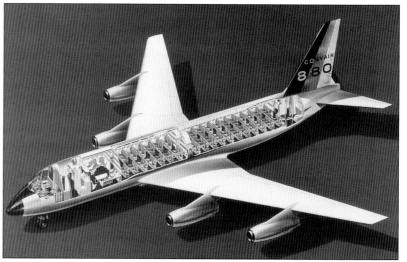

Cut-away drawing showing one of several proposed interior configurations for the 880. (General Dynamics)

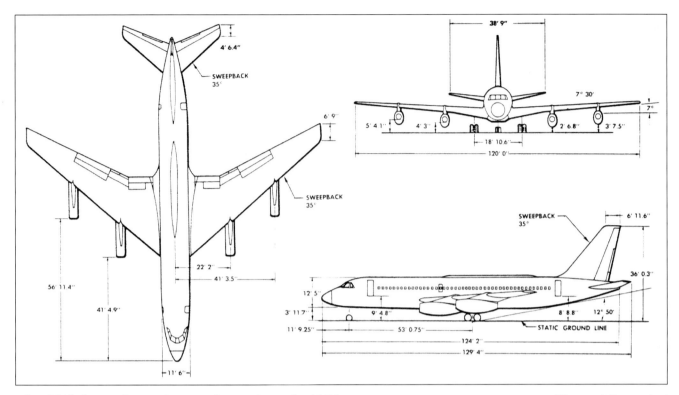

The 880's basic dimensions as drawn in early 1958.   *(General Dynamics)*

sistent hue because metal sections from different batches could not be exactly matched. Also, the rivets would still be silver. But this was a Howard Hughes idea, and no one was willing to argue the facts. Eventually Bob Rummel talked Hughes into a "best efforts" side letter on the matter, and it died quietly. Some interior metal trim appeared with the anodized gold color, including ash tray covers, door knobs and other appointments, becoming the only physical evidence of a unique idea.

By March 1957, the 880's maximum cruising speed had been increased to 615 mph, the result of a 10 percent increase in thrust — to 11,200 pounds — offered by General Electric's updated CJ-805-3 engine which replaced the -1 design. This light-weight single-spool, axial-flow, high-pressure-ratio power plant was designed for superior takeoff and cruise performance plus ease of maintenance and overhaul. Significantly, it would not require any thrust augmentation at takeoff, eliminating the need for a water injection system the early Pratt & Whitney models featured.

Other design changes included lowering the horizontal stabilizer from the vertical fin to the fuselage, with added dihedral, and moving the outboard engines further out on the wings. These and other modifications allowed a maximum takeoff weight increase to 178,500 pounds.

As the early phases of 880 tooling began at Plant One in San Diego, the last Convair 440s were being completed. Over one million square feet of floor space was available for the new jet program.

Convair engineers utilized a thicker aircraft skin — exceeding one-half inch in some locations — for resistance to crack propagation and to cut down on interior noise. This, in turn, reduced the number of fuselage support stringers. Fully duplicated hydraulic and cabin-pressurization systems were incorporated, but without power-assisted rudder or elevator control.

A "Scotchweld" system provided leak-proof, maintenance-free integral fuel tanks. Developed by Minnesota Mining & Manufacturing Co. (3M), it had first been used with great success by Convair on the F-102 fighter jet program. The company claimed there was no case on record of a fuel leak developing in an F-102. After careful cleaning and preparation, a film adhesive was inserted at all the tank joints, forming a complete bond when the wings were baked in an electric oven. Passenger windows were designed in similar fashion to the 707, two each per seat row, measuring 9 inches by 12.5 inches. Seat pitch was set at a generous 38 inches for both first-class and coach.

Cockpit window visibility was fairly good, especially when compared with propeller aircraft; both wing-tips were visible from either of the pilot's seats. The use of hot bleed air across the cockpit windshield replaced conventional wiper blades, another feature Convair developed for the F-102 fighter.

A dorsal fairing atop the airplane fuselage was added to house the Automatic Direction Finder (ADF) and Very High Frequency (VHF) communications antennas. The "speed bump," running from a point adjacent to the wings aft to slightly ahead of the vertical stabilizer, quickly became a visual trademark. Some have speculated that it was a design afterthought, but no evidence has been found to support such a theory.

Another unique feature visible of the 880 resulted from the plug-type passenger entry and galley service doors. Wedge-shaped in plan form, each door was designed to slide upward during the opening process, as the handle was rotated 180 degrees.

To save time, a decision was made to forego a hand-built prototype and instead use the first three production aircraft for the certification program.

Marketing Efforts

A full year after launching the program, substantial orders had not materialized. Only eight additional 880s had been spoken for. Transcontinental S.A. of Argentina ordered four in March 1957 on a conditional basis subject to completion of financing arrangements. REAL Aerovías Nacional of Brazil (later absorbed by VARIG) took four more in August. Convair found it almost impossible to sell 880s with the first 40 delivery positions already tied up by the Hughes agreement.

Among the most important target customers was United Air Lines, a prospect for up to 30 airplanes. It was also the largest U.S. carrier without Boeing 707s on order, opting instead for the Douglas DC-8. However, Boeing was already developing a light-weight 717 model designed to attract follow-up medium-range jetliner customers. It turned out to be larger than what United wanted, and lacked commonality with the Douglas jets.

In September 1957, United's board of directors authorized the purchase of 880s. Not to be outdone, Boeing quickly modified its 717 design to reduce size and capacity, turning out the medium-

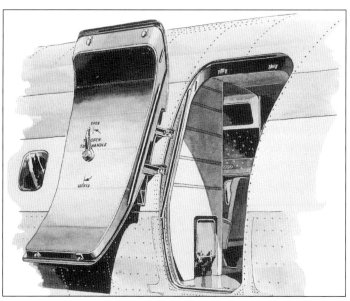

Fail-safe door design for the 880.   (General Dynamics)

range 707-020, with Pratt & Whitney's new lighter weight JT3C-6 engine. Coach seating would be six-abreast versus Convair's five-across layout and, for good measure, Boeing undercut the 880 price by $200,000 per airplane. Even as United's order was slipping away, Convair offered the JT3C-6 engine as an option on the 880, in November 1957, but it was too late. United ordered 11 Boeing jets and took options on 18 more. At the carrier's request, the designation was changed to "720."

In early 1958 Convair proposed a package for financially troubled Capital Airlines. It would not only cover the purchase of between nine and fifteen 880s, but also include the reorganization of an existing $48.5 million debt on Capital's Vickers

Viscount fleet. GD even went so far as to offer piston equipment leases to tide the airline over until its Convair jets arrived.

Capital's application for routes from Buffalo, Cleveland, Pittsburgh and Atlanta to points in Florida, originally supported by a Civil Aeronautics Board (CAB) examiner, was in jeopardy because the airline "had no suitable equipment on order" for the routes. Capital ordered four de Havilland Comet IV jets in 1956, but later canceled the deal. On January 26, 1958 a letter of intent to buy nine 880s was signed, and the routes were quickly approved.

Like United, American Airlines seemed to be more interested in the Boeing 720. As discussed later in this book, Convair went on to sell American a growth version of the 880 which would evolve into the 990.

Selling more 880s remained the primary goal of Convair's marketing department in mid-1958 when it turned to company engineers for improvements which might attract new customers. For the most part, foreign airlines had avoided the 880. With this in mind several design modifications were incorporated several months before the first basic airplane was completed.

The 880M

The new design became the 880-25, or Model 31, and was marketed as the "880M," with the M standing for "modified." Enhancements included:

Leading edge devices. To provide additional lift, four slats per wing were added — two each between the engine pods and outboard of the pods. There were also Krueger leading edge flaps between the fuselage and inboard engines, to provide proper airflow over the stabilizer on landing and takeoff. The cumulative effect

was a stall speed reduction of 10 percent.

Power boost rudder. An improvement over the basic 880's aerodynamic rudder, it allowed the pilot to maintain direction control more easily.

Increased engine thrust. CJ-805-3B engines with 11,650 pounds of thrust replaced the CJ-805-3 design, giving 4 percent better performance.

Greater fuel capacity. An added center section tank provided an additional 1,874 gallons of fuel. With the new 12,534 gallon total capacity, the 880M range increased 550 miles over the basic model, to 3,750.

Improved landing gear. To handle additional weight, a newly designed gear was incorporated.

The 880M was to be marginally slower than the standard version because the added operating weights, but both models were eventually certificated with identical speeds. Maximum fuel weight was increased 1,500 pounds over the basic model, to 121,500 pounds. This carried over in maximum takeoff weight, 191,000 pounds, and maximum ramp weight, 191,500 pounds. Allowable landing weight increased 10,000 pounds to 155,000 pounds (The higher landing weights were later upgraded on some standard models). Optional containerized cargo bins were offered but did not attract any takers.

880/880M Comparison (After certification)		
	880 (TWA)	**880M**
Empty operating weight	92,500 lbs.	94,000 lbs.
Max. ramp (taxi) weight	185,000 lbs.	193,500 lbs.
Max. gross takeoff weight	184,500 lbs.	193,000 lbs.
Max. landing weight	155,000 lbs.	155,000 lbs.
Max zero fuel weight	117,000 lbs.	121,500 lbs.
Fuel Cap. (US gal)	10,683	12,650
Normal cruise altitude	35,000 ft.	35,000 ft.
Service ceiling	41,000 ft.	41,000 ft.
Absolute Range (still air)	3,200 miles	3,750 miles
Engine thrust (sea level; pounds):		
CJ-805-3A	11,200	
CJ-805-3B		11,650
Maximum cruise speed:	610 mph*	610 mph*

* At 23,000 feet, equal to 393 knots indicated airspeed, 530 knots true airspeed.

This representation of airline customers was probably assembled in late 1958, showing several color schemes which never came to fruition. Swissair still appears as an 880 customer while Delta sports a DC-8-style livery and TWA reflects a pre-jet look.

Approach speeds for the M model declined from 191 mph to 179 mph, and the stall speed was reduced from 137 mph to 121 mph. Runway take-off length was also cut by about 1,000 feet, depending on weight and airport elevation.

The 880M cabin floors contained seat tracks to permit adjustment of the seat pitch, allowing increased capacity. The basic model's stationary lock-down positions restricted seating to a 38-inch pitch throughout the cabin.

The first 880M to fly, on October 3, 1960, was actually the house airplane, msn 1, modified to the new configuration. Type certification was received July 24,1961.

According to Bob Rummel, TWA and Delta pressured Convair for over a year during early 880 construction to add leading-edge flaps to the basic design. When the manufacturer finally agreed, the extra charge for Toolco's 30-plane fleet was set at $1.65 million, which Howard Hughes refused to approve. It is not clear whether this offer included all the M refinements. Delta declined also, perhaps considering the upgrade to be unnecessary for its needs. In any event, the TWA and Delta 880s were the only examples not produced as M models.

Limited Sales

A month after the CJ-805 engine received its civil certification on September 9, 1958, Swissair ordered five 880Ms and took options on six more. Delivery of the first airplane, for use on its South America and Far East routes, was scheduled for the fall of 1960. Two examples would be leased by Swissair to Scandinavian Airlines System (SAS).

The first 880 rolled out of Convair's San Diego plant in December and made its maiden flight on January 27, 1959. As of this date, the company still had only 53 on order.

Civil Air Transport of Taiwan opted for a single example in May, but further orders failed to materialize until October, when a formal agreement with Capital was finally completed for seven 880s, the first recognized order for the M model. An earlier deal between Howard Hughes and Capital was rumored, involving six of Hughes' block of 30, but it never came to fruition. On another occasion, the two parties reportedly negotiated for as many as 10 airplanes.

On October 7, Swissair announced an order for seven of Convair's new 600 model jetliners (see Part Two) and canceled its contract for five 880s. REAL also switched to the 600, and reduced its order from four to three.

Aerovías Venezolanas, S.A. (AVENSA) of Venezuela converted its letter of intent for a single 880M to a firm two-plane order in February 1960. Japan Air Lines announced a decision to purchase three, subject to government approval, and later ordered another two. Delta added three basic 880s to its original fleet, then four more, for a total of 17.

The balance of 880 sales came in single lots. Alaska Airlines bought an 880M. Hong Kong-based Cathay Pacific Airways initially purchased one from Convair, and eventually acquired eight more on the second-hand market. The U.S. Federal Aviation Administration (FAA) also bought a single M model.

Capital's 880 order became a casualty of the airline's merger with United Air Lines. The aircraft, already in various stages of assembly, were completed and sold, some after short-term leases. Transcontinental, S.A. was unable to finance its order and went out of business in November 1961.

Ship One was the last to be sold when TWA bought it in 1964. Only sixty-five 880s were built; 48 standard and 17 M models.

Above: *Practice roll-out of Ship One. In order to clear the hangar doors, the tail had to be lowered by placing the nose gear on a dolly.*

Right: *A retouched photo depicts the color scheme of Aerovías Venezolanas, S.A. The airline ordered a single 880 before merging its international routes with Linea Aeropostal Venezolana (LAV) to form VIASA.*

(both General Dynamics)

The Hughes Factor

Many credit Howard Hughes with the failure of Convair to attract 880 customers. His delaying tactics certainly cost the manufacturer precious time in the type's early development stage. Then his refusal to accept TWA's airplanes ran up individual airframe costs tremendously.

An example of the headaches inflicted came one day in 1959 when Hughes decided to test fly the 880 prototype. Convair had Ship One ready and a company limousine waiting at the Lindbergh Field terminal building. After a long delay, Lockheed's 188 Electra prototype landed and its crew, ignoring taxi instructions, pulled up behind the 880 and parked. Hughes, who had an Electra on order at the time and was negotiating for more, followed several men in flying suits down the airstairs, bearded and looking shabby with a rope for a belt and no socks. He walked over to N801TW, met chief test pilot Don Germeraad and boarded the Convair without delay.

Germeraad reported that Hughes, in the right seat, flew like he had several hundred hours in the airplane. They took the 880 out over the Pacific to perform stalls and other maneuvers. After a touch-and-go landing, Hughes declined Germeraad's offer of the left seat, commenting from the co-pilot's chair: "This is where I like to fly from." Continuing to shoot approaches at Lindbergh Field, the 880 disrupted traffic for over two hours, much to the distress of several airlines which incurred arrival and departure delays.

After the final landing, N801TW returned to its parking place next to the Electra. Hughes immediately reboarded the turboprop and was gone.

Clockwise From Top: *Ship One departing from San Diego.* **Lower Right:** *Flight Engineer's station.* **Lower Left:** *Standard 880 cockpit.* **Left:** *Members of Ship One's first flight crew pose after landing at North Island Naval Air Station on Coronado Island January 27, 1959. Left to right: R. B. Bloom, flight engineer, Donald P. Germeraad, pilot, B. B. Gray, second flight engineer, E. A. Davies, instrument engineer, J. E. Moroney, flight test engineer, and Philip M. Prophett, co-pilot.* *(General Dynamics photos)*

Right: *Convair claimed the title of "Home of the World's Fastest Jets" in 1959 with its B-58 Hustler, F-106, and 880.* **Center:** *The three 880s used for initial flight testing pose outside Convair's main plant.* **Bottom:** *The first 880s for launch customers TWA and Delta on the final assembly line.*

(General Dynamics photos)

Chapter Two
Initial 880 Airline Operations

Delta Air Lines, Inc.

Delta Air Lines represented a major success story for the 880, which it called the "Aristocrat of the jets."

On February 9, 1960, Delta president C. E. Woolman accepted N8802E during a ceremony at the Convair plant. Christened *Delta Queen,* it arrived at the company's Atlanta headquarters the following day after being intentionally routed via Miami for the purpose of establishing a transcontinental speed record. Under the command of Captain T. P. "Pre" Ball, the 880 flew 2,359 miles across the country in 3 hours, 31 minutes and 54 seconds, shaving 27 minutes off the old coast-to-coast record, set a month earlier by a Delta DC-8 delivery flight between Santa Monica and Miami.

Inaugural Convair 880 Royal Jet Service commenced over three routes on May 15, 1960. The first, Flight 870 (N8802E), departed Houston at 9 a.m. for New York-Idlewild, followed by Flight 873 (N8804E), 15 minutes later, on the New York-New Orleans route. That same day, Flight 883 (N8803E) flew from New York to Atlanta.

Nine 880s were delivered to Delta in 1960, permitting rapid expansion of jet service, despite the loss of N8804E in a

training accident. In addition to the inaugural routes, Dallas-Atlanta and Houston-New Orleans flights began July 1, followed by Chicago-New Orleans (nonstop and via Memphis) and Chicago-Atlanta on August 1. Houston-St. Louis-Chicago and Philadelphia-Baltimore-New Orleans-Houston service commenced October 30. In December, Chicago-Miami and Cincinnati-Miami flights were added.

In June 1961, Delta received new route authority to Las Vegas, San Diego, Los Angeles, and San Francisco as a result of the Southern Transcontinental Service Case. The 880s flew four

A wonderfully staged photo shows Delta's attractive all-first-class 880 interior complete with Dick Tracy comics.
(General Dynamics)

The first 880 to be received by Delta shows off its all-white livery. *(General Dynamics)*

Diego nonstop to Atlanta in 3:23:59 on May 11, 1960. An unofficial mark was set a month later, on June 11, when a New York-New Orleans segment took just two hours and nine minutes to complete. By mid-1962, the Delta 880 fleet held nine official speed records. Many of these will probably never be broken, as airspeed restrictions below 10,000 feet have since been implemented in the United States, slowing flights during the approach phase.

Delta was the only airline to utilize Convair's original suggestion for an all-first-class configuration, with 12 forward lounge seats and 72 in the main cabin. This arrangement lasted until December 5, 1961, when dual-class service began, with the introduction of 32 coach seats. The first-class cabin was reduced to 56 and its forward lounge was eliminated. As demand for coach capacity increased, the numbers continued to change, until a 24-72 ratio was achieved.

of the seven daily flights in this arena by mid-1962. The Caribbean destinations of Montego Bay and Caracas were added in December 1961 followed later by San Juan. The longest scheduled nonstop segment flown by Delta's 880s was between Los Angeles and New Orleans, a distance of 1,682 miles.

Several speed records were established during early Delta 880 operations. In addition to the initial delivery flight, another operated from San

The last four airplanes were received in mid-1962, allowing 880 service to be implemented at Newark, Jacksonville, and Detroit and expanded at existing Convair jet cities which grew to 24.

On March 29, 1972, Delta ordered fourteen 727-200s from Boeing. Part of the agreement called for the manufacturer to accept in partial

Delta standardized its livery with this DC-8-style design. *(Harry Sievers)*

Delta		
MSN	Fleet #	Reg.
04	901	N8801E
07	902	N8802E
11	903	N8803E
16	904	N8804E
17	905	N8805E
21	906	N8806E
29	907	N8807E
36	908	N8808E
38	909	N8809E
41	910	N8810E
50	911	N8811E
51	912	N8812E
52	913	N8813E
62	914	N8814E
63	915	N8815E
64	916	N8816E
65	917	N8817E

trade Delta's remaining fleet of sixteen 880s (reduced to 15 in December 1972, when N8807E was lost in a ground collision at Chicago-O'Hare). Deliveries of the Boeings commenced In January 1973, and a gradual 880 withdrawal began the following November.

With the soaring price of fuel, Delta decided to ground the fleet earlier than originally planned. All the Convairs were withdrawn by the end of 1973, then ferried to Boeing's Wichita, Kansas facility. The last two examples, N8810E and N8812E were handed over on January 14, 1974.

Delta's first-class seat pairs featured contrasting upholstery. (General Dynamics)

Northeast Airlines, Inc.

Although it never had a firm 880 purchase-order in place, Northeast became the second airline to operate the type, thanks to Howard Hughes, who released six of the 30 airplanes Toolco had ordered for use by TWA. General Dynamics, in turn, leased the airplanes to Northeast through a complicated agreement which delayed the program by several months.

Originally scheduled for delivery in mid-1960, the first 880 was finally handed over on November 30, 1960, just four days after its maiden flight. N8483H set a record time of 4 hours and 17 minutes en route from San Diego to Boston. The second aircraft, N8482H, followed on December 5, taking only two additional minutes to cover the same route. Four 880s were on hand when service was inaugurated on December 15 between Boston and Miami via Philadelphia. Fitted with 32 first-class and 65 coach seats, the TWA-configured 880s retained most original furnishings except for carpeting, upholstery, and new exterior color schemes. Northeast emphasized speed in its advertising for "the world's fastest jetliner."

Northeast		
MSN	Fleet #	Reg.
05	478	N8478H
08	479	N8479H
12	480	N8480H
20	481	N8481H
22	482	N8482H
23	483	N8483H
09	492	N8492H
18	493	N8493H
34	494	N8494H
39	495	N8495H

N8493H (msn 18) in Yellowbird colors at Philadelphia, only a few months before being withdrawn from service. **(Bruce Drum)**

In 1962, Howard Hughes, through Toolco, bought controlling interest in Northeast from the Atlas Corporation when the airline was on the verge of bankruptcy. No longer in control of TWA, Hughes had earlier been unsuccessful in his attempt to merge the two airlines. Two Toolco-owned 880s (N8494H, msn 34, and N8495H, msn 39) were delivered to Northeast in late 1962 for added lift but financial problems continued into 1963 and the company fell nearly $5 million behind on its payments for the six originally leased Convair jets.

Short of cash itself, General Dynamics had sold the lease agreement to a holding company for $20 million but, to complete the deal, was obliged to guarantee Northeast's payments. The airline began defaulting only two months later. Because it no longer held the aircraft titles, GD was stuck with the $5 million liability and no legal right to seize the airplanes. It wound up buying them back from the holding company in order to move for repossession.

Faced with foreclosure, Northeast agreed to gradually begin returning the six 880s. The first two (N8480H, msn 12, and N8483H, msn 23) were turned over in July, and immediately replaced by the remaining two Toolco airplanes (N8492H, msn 9, and N8493H, msn 18). The last four GD leased examples were returned by mid-September. Toolco replacement aircraft arrived at Boston with SuperJet titles, replacing 880 on the vertical stabilizer (N8483H was seen with this revision also, just

prior to being withdrawn). The four replacement examples may have had slightly different interior furnishings from the original six, however all were completed to TWA specifications. Cabin layouts eventually consisted of 24 first-class and 74 coach seats.

Toolco relinquished control of Northeast at the end of 1964, but continued the Convair lease arrangement. The 880s were repainted in Yellowbird colors following a corporate image update in 1966.

In 1968, new Boeing 727-200 aircraft joined the fleet (Northeast was the first airline to operate the type). The Convairs were withdrawn from service during January and February, then ferried to Marana, Arizona for return to Toolco, closing out seven years of 880 service with Northeast.

Trans World Airlines, Inc.

Following a lengthy start-up delay caused by Howard Hughes, TWA went on to operate the largest 880 fleet of any airline. Hughes relinquished all rights to nineteen of Toolco's 880s on December 30, 1960, his last day in control of the airline. Deliveries to TWA commenced two days later, with four Convairs accepted by January 18, 1961, in addition to one purchased earlier for crew training and route proving flights. The remaining airplanes, either completed or in final stages of production, were badly needed by the airline and readied as quickly as possible.

Eight-eighty service commenced from five cities on January 12, 1961: New York-Idlewild, Chicago-O'Hare, Phoenix, Las Vegas, and Los Angeles, followed by Dayton and San Francisco on January 20, and Kansas City nine days later. The longest nonstop segment was between Chicago and San Francisco.

Speed records began falling immediately. On January 24, an 880, averaging 680 mph, flew from Chicago to New York in 1 hour and 11 minutes.

TWA's Convair 880 "SuperJets" initially had an 85-passenger capacity, configured with 11 rows of four-abreast first-class seats plus a 12-seat first-class lounge

— six available for sale — and seven five-across rows in coach. After first-class passengers began complaining about being assigned to lounge seats, the left-hand portion was taken out and replaced by three two-seat pairs, reducing the actual lounge area to six seats, all on the right side.

Although the company's 880s were flown

A public relations photo curiously shows all-first-class seating in this TWA 880. *(General Dynamics)*

strictly on domestic routes, TWA contemplated basing a limited number overseas to operate intra-European and perhaps Asian flights from gateway cities. Reportedly, some of the airplanes were pre-wired at the factory for future high frequency radio installation. Whether this option was ever seriously considered has not been confirmed.

By the end of August 1962, Convair jets were serving 17 TWA cities. A near-transcontinental nonstop route had been added between Pittsburgh and Los Angeles.

In 1963 TWA purchased six 880s that had been operated by Northeast. All were built to TWA specifications under the original Toolco agreement and easily refurbished for fleet commonality. The first three were delivered on July 29 and all six had been received by September 13. Five-abreast coach seating was popular with passengers, and proved to be a competitive advantage in certain situations. TWA's "Briefcase Commuter Service" was cleverly advertised in business travel markets, with emphasis on "roomy, comfortable 2 and 3 seating *at low coach fares.*" When United Air Lines began its new One Class Red Carpet DC-8 service in 1963 with a similar five-across arrangement, TWA countered by placing 880s on the route, while American Airlines brought Convair 990s into the market. Even with only a $6 difference between One Class and coach rates, United was unable to compete, and eventually abandoned the arrangement system-wide.

TWA was able to end piston-powered passenger flights west of Wichita in October 1964 when 880s took over the last Constellation service between that city and Albuquerque via Amarillo.

The final 880 to be purchased was Convair's 'house' airplane, Ship One, which had been modified to M model standards for that type's certification program. Made available for purchase in 1964, it attracted TWA's interest, but the company wanted fleet commonality, which would require conversion back to the standard configuration from the M model. After negotiating with Convair, it was decided to do the work in-house. Re-registered N8489H, Ship One was delivered to Kansas City on October 29, 1964. Ninety-thousand man-hours and seven months later, it carried revenue passengers for the first time, on May 28, 1965, after being re-certified as a Model 22-1.

TWA had pulled the remaining first-class lounge seats out by 1962 and reduced premium seating to 32. With continued increases in the coach capacity — by this time 62, and later as high

With spoilers up, a TWA Convair rolls out at LAX. (Terry Waddington)

as 77 — a second aft galley was added. One 880 was sub-leased by Northeast to TWA in May 1967, for added lift during the busy summer season. N8495H, originally to have been N829TW for TWA, was instead retained by Toolco. While in TWA colors, it acquired, appropriately, fleet number 8829. To completely cover Northeast's Yellowbird markings, the entire belly and engine nacelles were painted gray, attracting a "Gray Ghost" nickname. Because of minor systems differences, it was assigned to a daily San Francisco-Detroit round-trip and flown by the same crews, although this was not mandatory, and a few calls were made at other cities. When repainted for TWA, no one remembered to remove the "Thank You for Flying

Northeast" message located on the spoiler undersides and visible during the landing roll. The free advertising was hastily painted out following some good-natured kidding from passengers.

Plans to replace the Convair fleet were announced April 25, 1973. TWA ordered seventeen Boeing 727-200s with options on 17 more; deliveries were to begin the following summer and stretch through 1975. The Convairs would be phased out gradually as new Boeings and Lockheed 1011s came on-line.

However, the energy crisis began to take a toll on airline operations soon after the 727 order was announced; immediate schedule cuts were imposed.

Burning nearly the same amount of fuel as a 707-331 with much greater capacity, the 880 flying time was reduced and most of the new 727 order was deferred.

Three Convairs were retired during the second half of 1973, and one had already been withdrawn in 1972. Eleven more came out of the schedule

Trans World		
MSN	Fleet #	Reg.
42	8801	N801TW
02	8802	N802TW
03	8803	N803TW
05	8804	N804TW
06	8805	N805TW
08	8806	N806TW
09	-----	N807TW*
10	8808	N808TW
12	8809	N809TW
13	8810	N810TW
14	8811	N811TW
15	8812	N812TW
18	-----	N813TW*
19	8814	N814TW
20	8815	N815TW
22	8816	N816TW
23	8817	N817TW
24	8818	N818TW
25	8819	N819TW
26	8820	N820TW
27	8821	N821TW
28	8822	N822TW
30	8823	N823TW
31	8824	N824TW
32	8825	N825TW
33	8826	N826TW
34	-----	N827TW*
35	8828	N828TW
39	-----	N829TW*
39	8829	N8495H**
40	8830	N830TW
01	8871	N871TW

* Toolco delivery - not flown by TWA
** Sub-leased from Northeast Airlines

in January 1974 with only six still flying by June 1. Flight 449 closed out TWA's 880 service June 15, operating from Chicago to Kansas City with N824TW.

The 25-strong fleet of 880s, in storage and for sale at Kansas City International Airport (MCI), attracted few interested parties. Frustrated by its inability to market the aircraft, TWA announced in September 1976 that if no buyers came forward by October 4, the Convairs would be "cannibalized" and scrapped.

N811TW (msn 14) was sold the following May and broken up on the premises, in a further attempt to motivate prospective buyers. TWA workers watched with amusement as the scrap dealer struggled to cut into the airplane. This same company had earlier dismantled a few 707s with little effort, but the 880's stronger frame and thicker skin did not give up as easily. The dealer claimed a loss on the project.

Finally, on June 13, 1977, TWA announced it had entered into a $3.5 million contract for the sale of all twenty-four 880s to North Star Maritime Corp. of Los Angeles. Actress Terry Moore, listed as the company's president, had claimed to be once secretly wed to none other than Howard Hughes.

The airplanes would be converted to freighters and fly principally in the Middle East. But the deal fell through when North Star was unable to finance the purchase and TWA kept a $100,000 deposit. The freighter plan did stir up interest however, leading other unnamed parties to pony up a $200,000 deposit, also forfeited to TWA.

Finally, Van Nuys, California-based American Jet Industries agreed in February 1978 to purchase 16 of the 24 Convairs for $2.4 million, including spares. The contract also provided an option on the remaining eight ships but it was not exercised. The last of TWA's fleet, completely stripped, was sold for approximately $5,000 per airframe and scrapped by the same dealer who had earlier tackled N811TW. This time he brought in much heavier equipment for the task.

Civil Air Transport

Designated the flag carrier of the Republic of China, Civil Air Transport (CAT) purchased a single 880M. The *Mandarin Jet,* pride of CAT's fleet, was

accepted at San Diego on June 5, 1961, becoming the first M model delivered.

On July 12, inaugural service commenced between Taipei and Hong Kong, followed by Taipei-Okinawa on July 14, and extended July 17 to Tokyo and Seoul. Manila and Bangkok were added later, plus a weekend service over the 24-minute cross-island run between Taipei and Tainan.

The traditional dragon figure, symbolic of China's continuing quest for knowledge, appeared on the airplane's nose. Its 94-seat (40-54) inte-

rior, the most elaborate of any passenger jet at the time, resembled an oriental palace. The Mandarin Jet was sold to Cathay Pacific, and delivered to its new owner on October 1, 1968. *(General Dynamics photos)*

Venezolana Internacional De Aviación, S.A. - (VIASA) KLM Royal Dutch Airlines

One of the early 880M customers was Aerovías Venezolanas, S.A. (AVENSA), then one-third owned by Pan Am. A single airplane was ordered in 1959, a year before the airline's international routes were merged with Linea Aeropostal Venezolana (LAV) to form Venezolana Internacional De Aviación, S.A., or VIASA. The new company retained the order, and added a second airplane, then leased from Convair one of the Capital batch, for a total of three.

The first aircraft was delivered August 1, 1961, and placed into service between New York and Caracas. Following arrival of the second example a month later, VIASA was able to establish 880 routes from Caracas to Miami, Maracaibo, and New Orleans.

VIASA/KLM	
MSN	Reg.
53(M)	YV-C-VIA
56(M)	YV-C-VIB
37(M)	YV-C-VIC

Seating included the 12-seat lounge, plus 44 first-class and 34 coach seats in the main cabin.

From early 1962, both -VIA and -VIB were chartered by KLM on an 'as needed' basis for its Curacao-New York service, to connect with KLM DC-8s bound for Amsterdam. "RENTED BY KLM" was painted on the port side, just aft of the rear passenger boarding door.

In 1963, VIASA's third aircraft (YV-C-VIC), leased from Convair, was delivered with VIASA colors on the left (port) side and KLM markings on the right (starboard) side. KLM chartered the airplane from VIASA for its Curacao-Miami flights beginning May 2, 1964 and extended the service from Curacao to Paramaribo, Surinam the following day. In August, ALM Antillean Airlines was formed out of KLM's West Indies division and also chartered 880s from VIASA to supplement its propeller equipment until DC-9-30s took over.

All three VIASA Convairs were withdrawn by the end of 1968, and sold to Cathay Pacific.

VIASA's 880M YV-C-VIC (msn 37) wore company colors on one side of the airplane, and the livery of KLM on the other. It is shown departing New York-Idlewild in August 1963.
(Harry Sievers)

Alaska Airlines, Inc.

As the jet age dawned, Alaska was financially strapped and unable to finance new equipment purchases. It even had to pass up on a deal with Howard Hughes to lease up to six 880s. Jets were desperately needed to compete with Pacific Northern Airlines, due to acquire Boeing 720s in 1962.

Accordingly, Alaska President Charlie Willis went with hat in hand to Convair and, in 1961, came away with a contract for one unsold 880M,

round-trip between Seattle, Fairbanks, and Anchorage in a mixed-class cabin configuration. To maximize its turbine advantage, the airline stretched reality by advertising "Four Jets Daily To Alaska." The single flight did indeed have four jet engines!

Murals depicting Alaskan scenes are visible in the Golden Nugget 880's first-class lounge.
(General Dynamics photos)

N8477H (msn 54), a deal probably enhanced by the opportunity for Convair to place its product in Boeing's hometown.

Alaska inaugurated "Golden Nugget" 880M service on August 30, 1961, featuring one daily

The cabin interior included attractive wall murals and a full first-class lounge, plus a draft beer bar and brass rail. In 1963, company engineers developed a way to increase cargo capacity during winter months when passenger traffic was light. The 12-seat lounge was temporarily replaced by specially built containers, used mainly to transport fresh produce. This reduced passenger capacity to 16 first-class and 68 coach.

For increased utilization, Alaska occasionally used the 880 on Military Air Transport Service (MATS) charter flights. It was also loaned to Japan Air Lines between trips, for pilot training at Moses Lake, Washington.

"Seventy-seven Hotel," as it became known, was sold to Cathay Pacific in 1966, as Alaska's first Boeing 727s were delivered. Employees, having grown fond of their first jetliner, were sorry to see it depart.

Swiss Air Transport Co., Ltd. (Swissair)

After originally ordering five 880Ms in October 1958, Swissair changed its contract a year later, opting instead for the 600, later known as the 990. The first of seven 990s was to be delivered in March 1961 and enter service on Far East routes in time for the busy summer season. When deliveries

were delayed, Swissair agreed to lease a pair of unsold 880s as a stop-gap measure. The two airplanes were furnished according to specifications originally laid down by Capital Airlines, including a 10-place lounge plus 20 first- and 64 economy-class seats.

The first example, HB-ICL (msn 43), was handed over to Swissair on August 11, 1961. On its way to Switzerland, the second airplane (HB-ICM, msn 45), established a new 880 distance record flying 3,855 miles nonstop from New York-Idlewild to Zürich on August 21-22, in 6 hours and 57 minutes.

Following familiarization training, the 880M was officially introduced September 10, on one of three weekly flights between Zürich and Tokyo, although it reportedly operated at least one service to London in August, substituting for Caravelle equipment. Different en route stops were made on each of the three services, and included Geneva, Athens, Beirut, Cairo, Karachi, Bombay, Calcutta, Bangkok and Manila. Middle East flights twice weekly on the Zürich-Cairo run and Zürich to London segments rounded out the ambitious schedule

As 990s entered service with Swissair in March 1962, the two 880s were withdrawn, and returned to Convair.

Japan Air Lines Co. Ltd.
Japan Domestic Airways

Japan Air Lines (JAL) ordered three 880Ms in the spring of 1960 for delivery a year later. Two additional examples were acquired in 1962, and a further three, initially obtained on lease, were eventually purchased, for a total of eight aircraft.

A ninth, on lease, was acquired via Japan Domestic Airways (JDA).

The first three aircraft entered service on October 1, 1961, replacing DC-6B and DC-8 equipment. All operated between Tokyo and Hong Kong. One flight made an en route stop at Okinawa, while the second called on Osaka and Taipei. The third example flew nonstop to Hong Kong, continuing to Bangkok and Singapore.

Originally planned for a 16 first-class and 59 coach configuration, the aircraft were delivered in 16-74 layouts, without a lounge. JAL's cabin interiors featured an attractive oriental garden theme. The silver-gray, first-class seat upholstery featured subdued chrysanthemum floral patterns; coach fabrics were sand-colored.

Two additional 880Ms were purchased, and received in June and July of 1962, permitting the introduction of Convair jet service on JAL's Silk Route to London via Asia, the Middle East. A proving flight arrived at London's Heathrow Airport on July 14, and regular service began in October.

A further three 880s were obtained on lease from Convair in 1963 and subsequently bought by JAL for a total of eight, all factory-delivered.

The last three Convairs were utilized mainly on domestic Japanese and Southeast Asia routes, allowing the further phase-out of piston aircraft.

The final unsold production 880M was leased by JAL on January 4, 1965, for use by its subsidiary Japan Domestic Airways (JDA), on the Tokyo-Sapporo route. When JDA was integrated into Japan Air Lines, the Convair joined JAL.

The company suffered three 880 hull losses, all during training exercises. One involved JA8030, still in JDA colors when it crashed.

As more fuel-efficient and larger-capacity equipment joined the fleet, JAL disposed of its Convair jets in 1970. Two were sold to Cathay Pacific, and the remaining six traded in to Boeing.

Above: *JAL's attractive 880 interior decor did not include a lounge area.* *(General Dynamics)*
Lower Left: *The only 880 to wear the colors of Japan Domestic Airways (msn 45) was lost in a training accident in August 1966.*
(Peter Keating via The Aviation Hobby Shop)

JAL/JDA			
MSN	Reg.	Name	(Translation)
57(M)	JA8021	*Sakura*	(Cherry Blossom)
58(M)	JA8022	*Matsu*	(Pine Tree)
59(M)	JA8023	*Kaede*	(Maple Tree)
60(M)	JA8024	*Kiku*	(Chrysanthemum)
61(M)	JA8025	*Ayme*	(Sweet Flag/Iris)
46(M)	JA8026	*Yanagi*	(Willow)
48(M)	JA8027	*Sumire*	(Violet)
49(M)	JA8028	*Kikyo*	(Chinese Bellflower)
45(M)	JA8030	*Ginza*	(a district in Tokyo)

Cathay Pacific Airways Ltd.

Hong Kong-based Cathay Pacific decided that the 880 was a good compromise between the Comet IV and DC-8, chiefly because of its passenger capacity; the DC-8 was too large and the Comet too small. The company was further influenced by Convair's generous offer of immediate delivery and a four-year payment plan.

A single example was acquired in 1962, and Cathay went on to acquire a total of nine 880Ms over an eight year period; the last eight were bought second-hand.

VR-HFS was delivered on February 20, 1962 and inaugurated Cathay's first jet service April 8, on routes from Hong Kong to Manila, Bangkok, Singapore, Taipei, and Tokyo. The airline's DC-6, DC-6B, and the last DC-4 in the fleet were retired by January 1963, leaving the 880 and two Lockheed 188 Electras.

The company fleet was all-jet by 1968, with seven Convairs. From an original 101 seat configuration (12 first-class and 89 coach), capacity was eventually raised to 119 to meet traffic demands. Cathay was the only airline to operate

Cathay Pacific	
MSN	Reg.
47(M)	VR-HFS
43(M)	VR-HFT
37(M)	VR-HFX
54(M)	VR-HFY
53(M)	VR-HFZ
44(M)	VR-HGA
56(M)	VR-HGC
58(M)	VR-HGF
60(M)	VR-HGG

regular 880 services into Australia, on the Hong Kong-Perth sector.

By 1970, the need for larger equipment prompted an order for Boeing 707s and the type eventually replaced Cathay's Convairs. Two were lost in accidents and the remaining seven airplanes were withdrawn by early 1975 and sold in a single lot to Miami-based International Air Leases, owned by George Batchelor.

Cathay's only factory-delivered 880 is seen at San Diego, still showing its msn on the fuselage. (General Dynamics)

Above: *Wearing a modified tail livery, VR-HFS (msn 47) pauses at its Hong Kong-Kai Tak home base.*
(Barney Deatrick)

Below: *Shown in its final colors, VR-HGG (msn 60) awaits a new owner at Miami International Airport*
(Bruce Drum)

Chapter Three
880 SUBSEQUENT OPERATORS

Terry Waddington collection

Airtrust Singapore	
MSN	Registration
44(M)	N48059
47(M)	N48060
54(M)	N48062
21	N8806E

Airtrust Singapore

Orient Pacific Airways of Ft. Lauderdale, Florida was founded by Johnny Fong, who acquired three Convair 880Ms from International Air Leases in late 1975. Initially based at Seletar Airport, Singapore, operations were conducted under the name Airtrust Singapore on a charter basis. Most flights carried oil drilling personnel between the Far East and drilling sites in Pakistan, Saudi Arabia, and Egypt. One aircraft (N48059) was based for a time during 1976 at Sharja, in the United Arab Emirates. During that same year msn 47 was written off in an aborted takeoff accident.

The remaining pair of 880s operated inclusive tour charters and scheduled flights for Air Malta towards the end of their careers, utilizing Orient Pacific flight crews. N48059 began this assignment November 24, 1976, followed by N48062 a few months later. The ships retained basic Airtrust liveries, minus titles.

Another 880, leased by a Greek company, Concordia, was ferried from the U.S. for additional lift. While not an Orient Pacific airplane, it was operated by Airtrust crews.

The Air Malta flights continued into 1979. A short time later, the Airtrust Convairs were ferried back to Singapore-Seletar and stored. Both were scrapped at that location in 1984.

Following its lease to Air Malta, N8806E was detained at Lisbon, Portugal on March 9, 1980, reportedly carrying arms bound for Karachi. It departed empty for Santa Maria in the Azores on May 4 but developed radio trouble and returned. The plane's captain took the malfunctioning equipment with him on a commercial flight back to the U.S., and did not return. Following several attempts to resolve the issue,  Portuguese authorities declared N8806E abandoned and sold it in 1985 for approximately $15,700. When the new owner was not heard from, an auction was conducted. Successful bidder Ribeiro Matias moved his acquisition about one kilometer from the airport and converted it to a bar and restaurant. The facility closed after several successful years of operation and now sits in a state of disrepair, although basically intact.

(Manual Rezende)

Air Viking

Charter operator Air Viking operated a single 880M (msn 48) under Icelandic registration for a short time during 1973. It is pictured at Keflavik shortly after being re-registered TF-AVB.   *(William T. Morgan)*

Lineas Aéreas de Nicaragua, S.A. (LANICA)

Above: *One of four 880s to wear the attractive colors of LANICA.*
Left: *N880JT was occasionally leased to LANICA while its own 880s were undergoing maintenance.   (Don Levine collection)*

Nicaraguan carrier LANICA acquired its first jet equipment in 1972, when Howard Hughes, via Toolco, exchanged two 880s (AN-BIA/BIB) for a 25 percent share of the airline. The first example went into service on July 14, 1972, between Miami, Managua, San Pedro Sula, San Salvador and Mexico City. Both aircraft were withdrawn in February 1975 and replaced by two ex-Delta 880s, which served LANICA barely two years before being retired in favor of Boeing 727 equipment. Another two Convairs were leased on short-term contracts in 1976 but not painted in full company colors. Records indicated that AN-BLX operated ad hoc services until June 1977 and therefore flew the last 880 service for LANICA.

LANICA	
MSN	Registration
39	AN-BIA
09	AN-BIB
04	AN-BLW
36	AN-BLX
61(M)	N5866
60(M)	N880JT

Above: *Four Winds, Inc. acquired msn 56 in September 1975. The company was later renamed Indy Air Travel Club.* (Phil Brooks)

Below: *Indy Air leased this 880M in late 1977.*
(via The Aviation Hobby Shop)

Rainbow Air attempted to start operations but apparently operated only one ferry flight, in early 1984, from Miami to Orlando-McCoy where the airplane was scrapped. (Bruce Drum)

Seattle-based Sunfari Travel Club acquired an ex-JAL 880M (msn 61) in 1972. (via The Aviation Hobby Shop)

Bahamas World utilized msn 7 for a short period of time in 1976, shuttling passengers to Nassau where they connected with low-cost flights to Europe.

(Michel Gilliand)

Freelandia Travel Club leased N1RN from 1973. *(ATP/Airliners America)*

This former TWA 880 (msn 32) remains stored at Mojave, still wearing a fictitious "Pan West" livery for filming of an Amazing Stories *television episode.*

(Jim "Jet" Thompson)

Another movie star, N812AJ (msn 23) was painted up in generic colors for the Warner Brothers production of The Rookie *in 1990. It still resides at Mojave.*

(Phil Brooks)

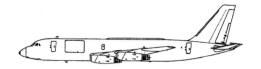

Chapter Four
880 CARGO CONVERSIONS

Latin Carga was based at Caracas and flew 880s in addition to DC-3s, C-46s, and other small aircraft. YV-145C (msn 64), the only 880 to wear full company colors, crashed at Caracas in 1980.

(Nigel Chalcraft)

The 880 became a logical candidate for main deck cargo conversions in the mid-1970s, when the TWA and Delta fleets came on the used airliner market.

In the summer of 1977, Miami-based Monarch Aviation purchased five former Delta 880s from Dwight Mercer's Aircraft Investors Retaining Corp. for conversion to freighters. Monarch advertised a $1.5 million modification package, which included installation of a 133-by-84-inch forward cargo door, floor strengthening, smoke and ground proximity warning systems, and a 9G crash barrier. The company accomplished full conversions on four of the airplanes at its Miami International Airport facility and completed all but a cargo door installation on the fifth.

N8813E (msn 52) was to be leased to Quisqueyana of Santo Domingo, in 1978, but the transaction did not take place, and the carrier ceased operations in 1980. The 880 is seen at Miami in its "new" orange & brown color scheme with Santo Domingo colors.

(Phil Glatt)

It also acquired other 880s for freight conversions. The aircraft went to carriers operating in Central and South America, and the Caribbean. It appears that, in most cases, these operators were either owned by or at least received financial support from Monarch. Three more Monarch-converted 880 freighters were lost in accidents.

As mentioned earlier, 16 TWA airplanes were bought by American Jet Industries (AJI), which was acquired by Gulfstream American Corporation (GA) in September 1978. Having nearly run out of Lockheed 188 Electras to convert, the company launched a sales promotion for its new "Convair 880 AirLifter."

Unlike Monarch, AJI worked very closely with Convair, and received its approval and full support, especially during

Photographer Larry Ivan Potoski was down to his last frame on Sept. 22, 1979 when the unbelievable appeared in his view finder. Monarch's N8816E was returning to Miami International with its cargo door fully open, proving how good the door hinges really were. This turned out to be slide number 38 on a 36-exposure roll of film!

the certification process. The AirLifter program promised a 51,000-pound payload for segments of up to 1,800 miles. Although substantially less than the 90,000-pound capacity of a new 707 freighter, its acquisition cost made the proposal sound attractive, and operating costs could be cut by cruising the 880 at lower speeds. AJI also offered a full spare parts support system for AirLifter customers.

In addition to the 16 Convairs acquired from TWA, GA had options on others but acquired only four — two each from the fleets of Delta and Toolco. At least one, and probably both, of the Delta ships received the Monarch conversion.

One of the Toolco airplanes (msn 18) became the first to be

converted at Van Nuys and was used for certification tests. The former N818TW (msn 24) also received the full treatment in California. The remaining Convairs were to be reworked assembly line-style at the Cooper Airmotive complex in Harlingen, Texas.

Unfortunately, the AirLifter program never caught on, and conversion work was halted. All the 880s were moved to Mojave, California for storage by 1980. A few had received partial modifications, but the conversions were not completed.

Only one GA-modified 880 actually carried freight in revenue service. Potter Aircraft, operating as the Flying Fish Company, flew msn 18 on Alaska charters in 1980-81 from Anchorage to Sitka, King Salmon, Kotzebue and Prudhoe Bay, where a 5,800-foot runway was utilized. The airplane later returned to storage at Mojave, where it remains, easily identified by a small fish painted on the tail.

The GA airplanes continue to languish in the California desert, except for a few disposed of over the years. In 1985, Charlotte Aerospace acquired the fleet and attempted to market them under its Caldwell Aircraft Trading subsidiary. By this time United States noise regulations prohibited 880 operations without sound suppression "hush kits," thus limiting sales only to foreign countries. Convair was approached on three occasions to explore possible re-engining. One of the

N880WA was purchased by Vincent Faix in August 1984, a few months before this photo was taken at Miami. The Convair hauled livestock towards the end of its career, and was broken up at Miami a year later. (Peter W. Black)

studies was quite extensive and concluded that such an effort was technically quite feasible, but with so few airplanes available, the development costs could not be justified.

Chicago-based Torco Oil Company bought up the remaining fleet in late 1993, intending to convert the CJ-805 engines from kerosene to natural gas fuel, for use at oil drilling sites; the airframes were to be scrapped. Several attempts to communicate with Torco have been unsuccessful, but legal problems are said to have prevented this plan from proceeding, and the fleet was again for sale. Recently the company has stopped entertaining purchase offers, apparently preferring to keep its Convairs on the books for financial reasons.

N880SR (msn 7), the original Delta Queen, *finished her days as a freight-hauler, and mysteriously burned up at Mexico City in 1983.*
(Don Levine)

One additional 880 was converted for freight use by General Air Services of Miami. N8805E (msn 17) received a main deck cargo door in 1982, although the company normally limited its modification services to other aircraft types.

Wearing similar liveries and photographed at Miami in 1977, Monarch 880 freighters N8815E (blue) and N8817E (red) were both lost in accidents.
(Photos by Don Levine)

Louisville-based Central American Airways operated 880M N54CP (msn 46) in full colors on cargo services beginning in 1980. A year later, the company acquired a standard model and operated both on behalf of Profit By Air, Inc. between New York-JFK and San Juan, Puerto Rico. Doing business as Profit Express and appropriately painted, the aircraft departed from each city at 2:30 a.m. with up to 46,500 pounds of cargo. Because of the Convair's narrow fuselage, cargo containers were not interchangeable with other aircraft, which made the service uneconomical and it was discontinued. (Bruce Drum)

N54CP in Profit Express colors.   (Phil Glatt)

N817AJ (msn 04), lacked white crown skin paint.
(Donnie Head)

Costa Rican cargo carrier SERCA flew a single 880 freighter on twice-weekly flights between Miami and San Jose with msn 50, N8811E. The airplane was eventually abandoned at Caracas, Venezuela, where it remains in derelict condition.
(The Aviation Hobby Shop)

Left: *Inair Panamá operated two 880 freighters. HP-821 (msn 41) was originally N8810E with Delta. It was damaged beyond repair March 29, 1980 at Panama City.*
(via The Aviation Hobby Shop)

Below: *N8811E, all white except for the Monarch emblem on its tail.*
(Bruce Drum)

Lower Right: *N8805E (msn 17) was converted to all-cargo in June 1980 by General Air Services and leased to Seagreen Air. It flew fish between cities in Alaska during summer 1982, then returned to fly in Central and South American charters out of Miami. Haiti Air Freight acquired the Convair in 1985 for a planned freight service between Port-au-Prince and Canada, but its range was insufficient to carry a profitable payload. The 880 never operated for this company and remains for sale at Port-au-Prince.*
(Bruce Drum)

Sunjet International planned to fly passengers to St. Maarten and St. Kitts but was unable to establish operations. It reportedly attempted to begin cargo service as well but no evidence was found to confirm the company ever got off the ground.
(Don Levine)

Left: *Fourteen 880s and a lone 990 rest in storage at Mojave.* *(D. Stewart)*

Below: *One of the Mojave 880s includes msn 40 shown with a cargo door installed.* *(Jim "Jet" Thompson)*

Below: *The curious Sterling X-Press appeared on msn 62 in May 1985.* *(D. Matthews via The Aviation Hobby Shop)*

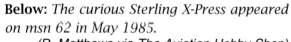

Above: *The former JA8027 (msn 48) ended its life at Mojave. Following FAA anti-misting fuel tests the Convair was broken up, still wearing this color scheme.* *(Phil Brooks)*

Chapter Five
The Odyssey Of N88CH

Following service with JAL and Cathay Pacific, msn 58 (M) became N88CH and received a luxurious executive interior in 1976 at Jet Aviation in Basle, Switzerland.

Acquired by Triple-D Corp. the Convair, named *Starship II*, carried Jefferson Airplane and other groups worldwide. It was bought by Ligonair in 1981.

Eighty-Eight Charlie Hotel was seized at MacArthur Airport, Islip, New York, for non-payment of tie-down fees and bought at auction by pilot Chad Koppie, who planned to land the Convair on his farm in Illinois. Following a brief legal battle, Ligonair re-acquired the plane and sold it to the Ciskei government in South Africa. When officials there refused to license the 880, it was bought by Billy Nels and transported to a site at Bonza Bay in East London. It now serves as Mr. Nels' private retreat, far from its San Diego origin.

N88CH seen at Stewart Airport, New York in 1978. (Tom Hildreth)

Jet Aviation via Georg Von der Mühl

Renamed Pinnochio *by its current owner, the green painted 880 blends in with its surroundings.*

Paul Goldschagg

Chapter Six
ELVIS PRESLEY'S *LISA MARIE*

Terry Waddington

Elvis Presley purchased msn 38 in 1975 for $1 million and spent another $750,000 for a luxurious new interior. Named *Lisa Marie* after his daughter and occasionally called *Hound Dog One,* it featured a queen-size bed, quadraphonic sound system, and lavish gold-plated bathroom fixtures. The TCB symbol with lightning bolt stood for "Taking Care of Business in a Flash."

The entertainer flew throughout the United States on "Eight-Eighty Echo Papa," including one trip to Hawaii, which added a navigator to the cockpit crew. In addition to interior upgrades, a portable ground power unit was stored in the forward cargo compartment, and could be winched out onto the ramp for electrical support at remote locations.

Following Presley's death in 1977, the airplane went on the market for $3.9 million, but eventually sold at a much lower price to LM Corporation (no connection with daughter Lisa Marie) and flew charters within North America and also to France and Switzerland. After a period of storage in Florida, the airplane was ferried from Florida to Memphis, Tennessee on February 6, 1984 and towed through the city streets to Presley's Graceland museum, where it remains on permanent display.

Interior photos courtesy Tom Sheridan collection

Chapter Seven
880 IN GOVERNMENT SERVICE

Originally a Convair 880M, msn 55, departing from San Diego for its first assignment, with the Federal Aviation Administration. *(General Dynamics)*

In 1958 — well before the first 880 rolled out — Convair made an elaborate presentation to the U.S. government, proposing a wide variety of military uses for its new jetliner. Projected designs included air command staff, special air mission, cargo-personnel, air evacuation, navigator-radar-bombardier trainer and refueler-tanker models. Another unique idea involved a crew trainer capable of simultaneous instruction of four B-58 Hustler three-man crews in flight. Sadly, the package was completely rejected, and none of the original military applications came to fruition.

The government's Federal Aviation Administration (FAA) did, however, purchase a single 880M for use in its flight safety program. For 18 years, msn 55, was based at the agency's Oklahoma City, Oklahoma headquarters, and flown barely enough to keep its crews qualified.

In 1980 the FAA's msn 55 began a new career with the United States Navy.

Featured at a 1985 Patuxent River open house, the immaculate UC-880 is pictured in its first U.S. Navy livery sporting extra antennas and other modifications. *(Tom Hildreth)*

The Amazing Convair UC-880

By Rich Lytle
former Navy UC-880 Program Manager
Force Warfare, Naval Air Test Center
Patuxent River, Maryland

Amost unique addition to the Navy's inventory was the Convair 880 model 22M, modified for in-flight fueling with a 75-foot hose and drogue, and Tomahawk cruise missile operational testing. It was used for verification and support of unusual projects with both the FAA and Navy for its entire career. Designated "UC-880" with military tail number 161572 assigned, this aircraft was supported by a team of dedicated contract pilot and maintenance personnel who kept the aircraft mission-ready long after all other Convair 880 aircraft had ceased flying. Flight Systems, Inc. (FSI), based at the Mojave Airport in California, installed and tested the refueling system, certified by Naval Air Test Center (NATC) engineers, and initially provided the flight crew and maintenance team that operated out of the NATC facility at Patuxent River, Maryland. Until struck from the Navy inventory of active aircraft in September 1993 it maintained an enviable state of readiness in support of Naval aviation's highest priority programs.

The UC-880 was routinely dispatched to Elgin Air Force Base (AFB) in Florida and Naval Station Roosevelt Roads, Puerto Rico with several Navy fighters in tow, providing a nonstop in-flight refueling capability as necessary. It flew missions to remote areas in support of fleet activities as far away as Adak, Alaska and the eastern Mediterranean, based in Egypt.

In spite of the numerous modifications to the basic airframe which included installation of a KA-3 "Whale" air-to-air refueling package, large and small antennas (one of which induced significant mach buffet/airspeed and altimeter errors at high altitudes and speeds) and a complete suite of electronic equipment aft of the flight deck allowing 12 specialists command and control for missile telemetry/control, etc., the high stress maneuvers during the cruise missile chase and other airborne projects provided more than enough testimony to the flight deck crew to convince them of the unusual structural integrity of this aircraft. (The altitude and airspeed errors were later eliminated by providing a switch the pilot would move to an alternate position after takeoff, causing the pitot static system to use a different set of static ports on each side.)

The final test of the UC-880 was completed December 9, 1995 and sponsored, ironically, by the FAA which originally operated the aircraft from factory delivery until 1980. This highly successful test, one in a series to provide a data base for aircraft vulnerability to explosive charges, was the first involving an aircraft with all systems operational, simulating an internal explosion at high altitude. Amazingly, the 880 with its unique flight control systems design retained limited flight control authority, using emergency backup systems and trim.

The UC-880 and its sister ship will soon be headed to the scrap heap to be "salvaged" for aluminum content. The end of these two aircraft coincides with the recent closing of Convair's plant in San Diego. Back in 1959 this company boasted that it made the fastest fighter (F-106), fastest strategic bomber (B-58 Hustler) and the fastest jetliner, the amazing Convair 880.

(U.S. Navy photo via Tim Averett)

Top: *The UC-880 (msn 55), affectionately known as* Old Smokey, *awaits her destiny, following tests at Pax River.*

Above: *N48063 (msn 56) was acquired by the Navy as a source of spare parts. It is seen at Miami prior to retirement.* (Tom Sheridan)

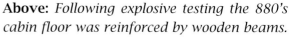

Above: *Following explosive testing the 880's cabin floor was reinforced by wooden beams.*

Left: *Still looking good, Old Smokey was retired with total flight time of only 12,267 hours.*

(UC-880 photos by Rich Lytle)

A Tribute To The 880

By Paul W. Bennett

Author's note: The following story, written by a Delta Air Lines pilot, first appeared in the January 1974 edition of Delta Air Lines' in-house newspaper Delta Digest, *shortly after the company's 880 fleet was retired. This sentimental remembrance is reprinted in its entirety, with thanks to Delta for permission to do so.*

London: "Earth Systems, Inc. reported yesterday the sale of fifteen aluminum alloy capsules to Energy, Inc. of New York. The containers will be used for the disposal of dangerous radioactive wastes in outer space. They were reportedly chosen for their mission because of their virtually indestructible outer shell, an apparent result of years of exposure to extremes of temperature and humidity in the lower atmosphere, a process not really understood by present day science. Origin of the capsules is obscure, but an informed source suggests they may have once served as commercial air transport vehicles during the early jet era."

From a report in
The World Journal, January 11, 2063

We were carrying about 10 knots over the minimum approach speed, and the airplane was behaving nicely, but about two miles off the runway it became apparent we were undershooting the field. "You're low," Sandy said, and my response might have been, "You don't have to tell me, I can see that," but I tell you I was too busy to respond.

In the early '60s, the jets were launched, and the jet era had begun, but, let's face it, few of the major airports were really equipped to receive them. For one very important thing, many lacked that most essential landing aid, the Instrument Landing System, on some of the best runways. For the uninitiated, the Instrument Landing System, or ILS, consists of a localizer beam to guide the pilot down to, and along the center of, the runway; and, perhaps more importantly, the glide slope, which directs the aircraft downward at such an angle that it arrives over the runway at a prescribed elevation. Sort of like driving down a hill on a very narrow road entering a tunnel at the bottom. This guidance system is of course only part of the whole picture of shooting the approach; the pilot must also maintain a specific airspeed, sinkrate, etc. What is sinkrate? How fast you are approaching Mother Earth.

Anyway, we were low because, as I mentioned, if you are to pilot a jet, you must have specific information from these landing aids, and brother, there just weren't any on that runway. Just a case of eye-balling it, and jockeying the power a bit, and thumbing the beep trim a little, and watching the sinkrate and airspeed all the while you are coordinating your control inputs with your instrument readouts. "Like milking a mouse," the late Lee McBride put it. Easy, you say. But with your instruments flying?

Now when you cannot believe what you see, it fills you with a certain dismay, meaning you know something's wrong that you cannot immediately identify. So you fall back on certain basic instincts. I thought, "The spoilers are up," so I applied power and rotated, and called for go-around flap and gear up, and we pulled out. I turned my head slightly, and said to Tex, "Dump 10,000 pounds," and he was opening the fuel jettison valves even as I spoke. Because, you see, Tex was, like Sandy, "in the loop." And he dumped fuel all over southwest... very efficiently and quickly with no reservations about kerosening the area. Bless his heart.

Sandy was Sandy Sandridge, and Tex was Tex Kilcrease, first and second officers in my crew. Pleased to meet you. You know the gentlemen? A pleasure.

We never really found out about that airplane, other than a minor problem with the pitot-static system which maintenance fixed. But I suspect Gremlins, and I'm not referring to the variety which gives American Motors an operating profit.

The airplane was, of course, that beautiful, intricate, sophisticated, temperamental, perfectly marvelous, very rapid, and sometimes logic-defying vehicle known as the Eight-eighty. Ever flown in one? No? What a pity!

The 880 was many an airline pilot's first jet, certainly mine, and like Arthur Murray, it taught you lots in a hurry. Like the prerequisite of the ILS to aid you in spotting 75 tons of aircraft where it should be spotted, after boiling in over the fence at a charming 140 knots or so. Like the business of "going around;" power, rotation, flaps, gear, etc. — in flight training you did it properly and positively, or you didn't do it at all. And speaking of flight training, who in the ranks of 880 pilots can forget his first takeoff at the controls of an 880, after a lifetime of operating a piston? The noise, the absolutely unbelievable surge of power, the breathtaking acceleration of this awful fire-breathing monster? And the instructor pilot's final quiet admonition; "If you lose an engine, for God's sake don't push the wrong rudder." For a *V1* cut (losing an outboard engine at a critical point on takeoff) in an 880 was akin to being sideswiped in a Volkswagen by an express train; if you didn't react properly, you might find yourself racing across the runway and out into the boondocks, the road far behind. And who can forget one's initiation into the mysteries of the "Dutch Roll," that perfectly awful display of bad manners so unique to the 880? And the "emergency descent" from 35,000 feet, reminiscent of acrobatics in the Old Days? Let's see, power off, spoilers up, gear speedbrake down, a 40 degree bank and pushing the nose down below the horizon, and the airspeed coming up fast toward the barber pole, and the sinkrate gone insane, and again the instructor's final admonition; "Be sure you don't overspeed, because that will ring the bell and you aren't allowed to ring the bell, but anyway we have already fouled it up, you didn't don your oxygen mask, let's go up and try again. And this time you must remember to advise ATC you are having an emergency descent, and also don't forget to instruct the flight engineer in how to handle that electrical fire that brought this on in the first place."

Speaking of the "Dutch Roll," do you know about that? In this perfectly absurd maneuver, invented for (or by) the 880, the wings begin to wobble, and the nose begins a yawing left and right, all out of coordination one against the other, and if you don't put a stop to this in a hurry you will soon be wishing you had checked out in someone else's airplane. I remember when I was up for checkout, I went quizzing the 880 pilots about the airplane, and they were really enthusiastic, until I got to the point: How do you handle the Dutch Roll on climbout? And then they would look away and be sad. But then somebody discovered how to "pop the spoilers" and that took care of that. But let me tell you about the 880 — there was no waltzing around with that queen.

Incidentally, the 880 was christened the Delta Queen, remember? Following hard on the Royal Crown DC-7, the name was appropriate, I suppose. But somehow I never liked the name. Queen signifies haughty, aloof, possessing the feminine mystique. The 880 isn't and doesn't. It is, as I said, deliberate, brawny, certainly very rapid, and thoroughly masculine in all its movements. Some have said it is noisy and dirty. But feminine it isn't. A passenger told me he preferred the 880 because, in his words, "an 880 flight is as close as I'll ever get to ride in a fighter plane." Another, when I asked what pleased him most about it, remarked "that gut feeling one gets every time the landing gear slams up

into the fuselage." Certainly, it had more than its share of Machismo, let us say.

The 880, of course, was a product of the Convair division of General Dynamics in San Diego. Conceived during the mid-50s as a super-fast luxury medium range transport, in early 1959 the aircraft was first test-flown with gratifying results. Many issues of the DELTA DIGEST during that period were taken up with ongoing reports on its progress. In the September 1959 issue, it was reported that "after six months of extensive flight tests, the 880 exceeds all performance estimates." Much praise was heaped on the reliability and good performance of the General Electric CJ-805-3 engines, and mention was made of the certified field length for landing on only 5,350 feet (!), using brakes only and no reversing. In the November issue, the DIGEST reported the public verdict already in on the noise factor as "loud but not annoying, with the engines' sound suppressers holding the noise level to no more than that of a four-engined piston transport." Other DIGEST issues spoke of the 880 as having "speed, luxury, and the best economics on the world's medium-range routes." Someone thought it was "an airline's dream," and our beloved Mr. Woolman himself called it a "sweet airplane." On its maiden flight, the 880 set a Southern Transcontinental speed record, making the run from San Diego to Miami in 3 hours and 32 minutes, for an average speed of 665 mph, with Captain Pre Ball in command; other crew members being Dick Tidwell, Maryanne Kowaleski, and the late Jim Longino. Soon followed a succession of new services over the Delta system, with most of the 880s being employed on the most highly competitive routes. Customer response was gratifying.

Certainly no account of this airplane should ignore its unique position in the airline industry. I say unique, for after all, only a few dozen were built: Delta ordered 16, TWA 42, I believe, and the foreign operators a scant few. American operated the Convair 990 (a faster version of the 880) for a while, but phased them out early. The 880 might have been even more singular had it been delivered as originally planned: that is, fabricated out of gold-colored aluminum alloy. But the idea was discarded, and it came on stage pretty much as we now see it. But just imagine — a solid gold airplane!! Then too, one might ponder how many might have been built, had the Boeing 727 not come on stream in such an avalanche of jets during the "soaring sixties."

The 880 also enjoyed certain other dubious distinctions. What other aircraft in history ever entered the downwind leg at a major airport "on the barber pole" (as fast as it could go), crossed the outer market inbound at 250 knots airspeed, and made a perfectly normal landing — with a horrified FAA inspector aboard? As the story went, the inspector took no action and failed to report it, because "nobody would believe it happened!" For all its speed — it led the pack — the 880 could be slowed in a hurry, being equipped with all sorts of arresting devices. This perhaps prompted some pilots to look on it as a real hot rod to be operated as such, and "speed records" were broken almost daily. "Maybe the devil made 'em do it!" But then new speed restrictions were put into effect, and wiped all that out. The 880 also may have signaled the coming of the "Age of Aquarius" long before Broadway. Remember, it was once pumped full of water by an over-zealous ramp service attendant. Remember, too, the passengers were treated to a full-scale tropical downpour in the cabin when the electric fan was turned on!

What really characterized this airplane was its rare mix of utility, inherent good looks, and swift way of going about its business. Perhaps something about it raised the spirit a little — one could say it was pleasurable just to observe its lean and hungry look while parked at the ramp or awaiting takeoff. Most aircraft offer their best profile in flight, sans wheels, flaps, etc. hanging out — but the 880 had flair even in that earthly con-

dition. Given his choice of aircraft, would not Columbus have chosen the 880 for its elegance, as well as its promise of a swift crossing? And through its use, would not the message to Garcia have been delivered with more promptness?

And surely the 880 has worn well. Over the years, it has performed successfully and honestly at its assigned tasks. Like the thoroughbred it is, it started fast, ran a beautiful race, and finished in the money. It had class.

But this isn't the end of the line. My friend who can see into the future tells me this noble ship will be around a long time. It will serve in other hemispheres and under other nation's colors. In our world there are veritable millions of people waiting for their first jet experience. Where will it be? South America, Africa, the Orient? I can't say, but I may have a clue. In a dream recently, I was propelled forward into time, and found myself attending a 1995 meeting of the International Brotherhood of Airline Pilots. We were gathered in a great hall with pilots from every corner of the earth. This one pilot was speaking to me in Chinese with great fervor and enthusiasm. I neither speak nor understand that language (!), so each time he spoke I shook my head negatively. He finally sighed and fell silent. At this moment, an interpreter offered to help. "What does he say?" I queried. "He says," the interpreter answered, "'Ever flown an 880? Ever flown in one? No? What a Pity!'"

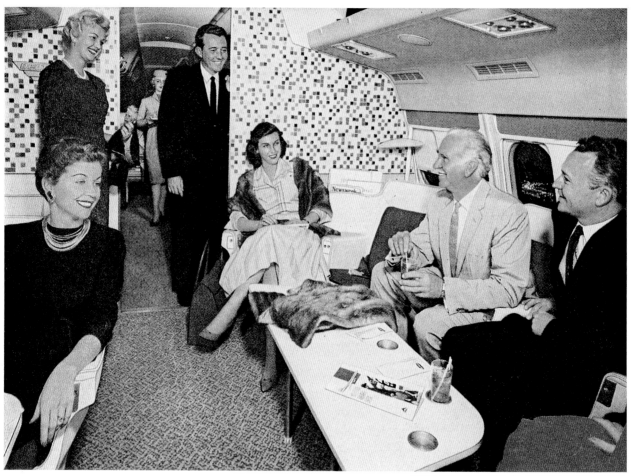

CLUB COMPARTMENT OF DELTA'S CONVAIR 880

The fastest, quietest, most luxurious jetliner travel in all the world is now available as new Delta Convair 880's link New York non-stop with Atlanta, New Orleans and Houston...Atlanta with Dallas...*Chicago with Atlanta, Houston, Memphis, New Orleans. Eighteen major cities will soon be on Delta's Convair 880 and DC-8 jet routes.

*STARTS JULY 1

DELTA ▶
AIR LINES
The air line with the BIG JETS

A Slightly Modified 880....

When the United Air Lines order for thirty 880s was lost at the end of 1957, drastic measures were taken by Convair. In order to sell jets to American Airlines, the company was willing to make major changes to its jetliner design. American desired something with a transcontinental range and greater speed. Its legendary president C.R. Smith wanted to operate an all-first-class "Blue Streak" coast-to-coast nonstop service which would be up to 45 minutes faster than the competition. If Convair could meet this need, Smith would make a purchase.

Negotiations began in early 1958 and in August produced an order for 25 airplanes, to be called the Convair 600. American also announced the purchase of 25 Boeing 720s powered by conventional Pratt & Whitney JT3C-7 turbojet engines.

Incredibly, Convair's contract with American to build what amounted to an almost completely new air-

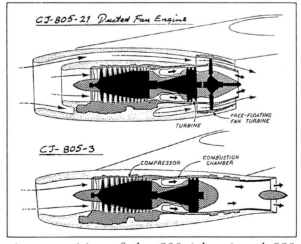

A comparision of the 600 (above) and 880 (lower) power plants.

plane was signed without approval from General Dynamics' board of directors. Afterwards, the board was informed that there would be "a slight modification" to the 880 design. Directors must have been somewhat confused a short time later, when the 880M variant surfaced.

Enter The Turbofan Engine

To meet a 635 mph speed requirement Convair turned to the new "turbofan" engine design which would provide a substantial power increase. While Pratt & Whitney was developing a power plant with the fan component mounted on the front end, General Electric proposed a basic upgrade of the existing CJ-805 used on the 880, and could minimize development time by placing the fan at the rear, which also made possible a higher bypass ratio. The 600 would be first transport designed specifically around a turbofan engine.

The new G.E. CJ-805-23 incorporated an additional turbine and fan combined

Above: *Convair's new design featured fatter engine pods and unique wing-mounted anti-shock bodies.* **Below:** *The outer anti-shock body fuel dump chute can be seen along with the unmodified engine nacelle.* (General Dynamics photos)

in a single stage or wheel, with no mechanical connection to the main engine rotor. The inner circle of the wheel was composed of turbine blades turned by the jet exhaust. Near the circumference of this wheel the turbines became fan blades which pulled air around the basic engine, exhausting it through a double jet nozzle at low velocity, thus improving engine efficiency by up to 40 percent. Its standard day thrust at sea level was 16,050 pounds. A clam-shell type reverser system, similar to the 880, was selected.

Because mixing of the aft fan exhaust with the basic jet engine exhaust achieved sound levels comparable with that obtained by use of a sound suppresser on conventional jets, the CJ-805-23 could be operated without such a device. As with the non-fan CJ-805, water injection was not required.

A unique engine pod was designed to include an inner cowling structure immediately around the engine, plus an outer cowl to form an air duct for the aft fan. The double cowling structure retained the standard bottom-opening feature of a single design for ease of maintenance. Access to the engine was gained by raising the outer pod doors, then the hinged ducts.

By adding a 114-inch section amidship, the 600 fuselage could accommodate 123 passengers in an all-coach layout, or 137 in high-density seating. All-first-class capacity (including six lounge seats) was set at 98. A variety of dual-class configurations were also offered.

Area Rule Design

The most unique physical change in the 600 design came with the introduction of four anti-shock bodies on the trailing edge of its ultra-thin wing, which was swept back 39 degrees. Utilizing the modified "area rule" concept developed by Richard Whitcomb of the National Advisory Committee for Aeronautics, these pods, which resemble inverted canoes, were added to take a continuous air flow over the upper wing surface and lessen or delay the shock wave which increased drag at speeds between Mach .80 and Mach 1.0. This configuration optimized the lift/drag ratio and allowed an economical increase in cruise speed. The wing area was 250 square feet greater than the 880, and leading edge slats were added between the inboard engine pylons and wing tips. The size and num-

ber of anti-shock bodies could be varied for convenience, and Convair finally settled on four — two on each wing — after experimenting with between two and 18. When the design was finalized, engineers found the pods useful as integral fuel tanks, boosting overall capacity to 15,562 gallons. Discharge nozzles were installed in the trailing edge tips of the pods for immediate fuel jettisoning without imposing a drag penalty.

Although structurally similar to Convair's 880, the 600 would become the first jet transport to be equipped with a new proportional anti-skid braking system, designed to increase or decrease pressure gradually and always apply maximum braking just short of the skid point on slick runways. Its landing gear was beefed up to allow heavier operating weights, and could be lowered at speeds of up to Mach .83 for emergency descents. The main gear strut was 10 inches longer than that of the 880 and attached lower in the wing structure. As a result the airplane stood approximately 18 inches higher at the main gear and sloped between one and two degrees downward toward the nose.

A full-power, hydraulically operated rudder control system was incorporated. This enhancement, along with the airplane's increased length, helped to minimize asymmetric takeoff thrust problems originally encountered on the 880. The 449-square-foot horizontal stabilizer represented an increase of 100 square feet over the 880.

A Hard Bargain

The 880's new big brother seemed to have a bright future, with its superior speed and launch order from American Airlines. However C.R. Smith, sensing Convair's urgent desire to sell jets to his company, had extracted a very attractive agreement in exchange for his business. In fact, it was too attractive.

Unless Convair could spread costs out over a long production run, it would surely lose money on the 600, although the amount could only be guessed, as the manufacturer had not yet determined what it would cost to build the airplane.

American's purchase price for twenty-five 600s was $100 million. Instead of a cash down payment, Convair agreed to accept twenty-five DC-7s in trade, at an assigned value of $22.8 million, easily dou-

ble the market value and thus reducing the 600 purchase price to just over $3.5 million per unit. Convair further agreed to sell the airline spare parts on an as needed basis and not charge for inventory storage.

Finally, as part of what it called a "mission guarantee," Convair certified the 635 mph speed with a partial refund of the purchase price should it fail to deliver. Also promised was the ability to fly 600s between close-in LaGuardia Field in New York and Chicago's Midway Airport. Both had notoriously short runways but, it was calculated, reduced weights required for such a stage length would be low enough to allow operations without a payload penalty.

Sales Drought

In 1959 it appeared Pan American World Airways would order 600s for its South American routes. A month later, during the CAB Southern

880/880M/600 Comparisons
As of April 1959

	880	880M	600
Wing span	120 ft.	120 ft.	120 ft.
Length	129 ft. 4 in.	129 ft. 4 in.	139 ft. 5 in.
Height	36 ft. 4 in.	36 ft. 4 in.	39 ft. 6 in.
Wing area	2,000 sq. ft.	2,000 sq. ft.	2,250 sq. ft.
Max fuselage width	11 ft. 6 in.	11 ft. 6 in.	11 ft. 6 in.
Max cabin width	10 ft. 9 in.	10 ft. 9 in.	10 ft. 9 in.
Cargo capacity (cu. ft.)	863	863	928
Empty operating wt.	89,000 lbs.	94,600 lbs.	113,000 lbs.
Max. taxi weight	185,000 lbs.	204,000 lbs.	239,000 lbs.
Max. gross takeoff wt.	184,500 lbs.	203,400 lbs.	238,200 lbs.
Max. landing weight	132,800 lbs.	155,000 lbs.	180,000 lbs.
Max zero fuel weight	117,000 lbs.	126,000 lbs.	149,000 lbs.
Fuel Cap. (US gal)	10,770	13,870	15,110
Normal cruise altitude	35,000 ft.	35,000 ft.	35,000 ft.
Service ceiling	40,000 ft.	40,000 ft.	40,000 ft.
Payload			
First-class	23,150 lbs.	23,150 lbs.	25,120 lbs.
Coach	26,780 lbs.	26,780 lbs.	29,245 lbs.
Range (statute mi.; F/C)	3,450	4,210	4,400
Engine thrust (sea level):			
CJ-805-3	11,200 lbs.		
CJ-805-3B		11,650 lbs.	
CJ-805-21			15,000 lbs.

Transcontinental Service Case hearings, Continental Airlines announced it would acquire four 600s if awarded new routes from Albuquerque and El Paso to the West Coast. Fall 1961 delivery positions had been negotiated along with a $20.2 million price tag including spares. Continental won rights from El Paso, San Antonio and Houston to California, but opted for turbofan-powered Boeing 720Bs instead. Ironically, Pan Am acquired the same type, second-hand, for Central and South American flights.

A proposed swing-tail 600 freighter was marketed but attracted little interest from military and civil customers. In addition, records indicate that marketing proposals were made to, among others, Aerovías Panamá, Air Jamaica, Pakistan International, Philippine and Tasman Empire Airways.

After signing up Scandinavian Airlines (SAS) for two 600s in September, a Swissair transaction the following month netted only two new airplanes; the carrier dropped its five 880 orders in favor of seven 600s.

In the spring of 1960 Convair, reportedly at the request of American Airlines, agreed to change the 600 designation to "990," although the new name was not publicly acknowledged until November. Some have said that 990 was chosen because it equaled the plane's cruising speed of 615 mph in kilometers but, at the time, the 635 mph was still promised. A more logical explana-

tion would be the desire to eliminate any impression that the new jet was inferior to the 880. The intercontinental version would later acquire the name "Coronado" from Swissair, recognizing the Spanish explorer and geographical location in San Diego, adjacent to the Lindbergh Field plant.

VARIG of Brazil inherited a Convair order originally for 880s, when it absorbed REAL-Aerovías in May 1961. After a dispute and several changes in the contract, an agreement for three 990s emerged prior to the VARIG takeover.

The Last Hughes Deal

The ubiquitous Howard Hughes ordered six 990s on September 10, 1960 when Convair agreed to take a like number of 880s from Toolco's commitment and lease them to Northeast Airlines. Hughes was said to have extracted a promise from

990 Ship One being towed to the flightline for taxi tests prior to its first flight.
(General Dynamics)

Convair not to use a number higher than 880 for any follow-up models, and it is assumed he acquiesced with this order. A year earlier, Convair had been enticed with the prospect of a much larger order, and 36 delivery positions were reserved for Toolco, starting in the second half of 1961. According to Bob Rummel, the negotiations were merely a ploy to extract better financing for the 880s which were nearly ready for TWA.

Even when the firm order was placed, Hughes must have known he would never take the airplanes, as all were to exactly match American's specifications. Toolco ordered seven more 990s in February 1961, over a year after Hughes lost control of TWA. None of the airplanes, to have been the last 13 off the line, were built. The total order was canceled in January 1962 as part of yet another complicated deal. Toolco's progress payments on the 990s exceeded by $7 million the price of its last four 880s, which had still not been accepted by Hughes. Under the agreement, Toolco took delivery of the 880s (which later were leased to Northeast), plus $1.5 million in cash and a promissory note for another $2 million. The $3.5 million balance was forfeited as a cancellation fee, but Howard Hughes still walked away with money in his pocket, which must have left GD executives shaking their heads.

Pratt & Whitney Catches Up

Although considered a year and a half behind General Electric in turbofan evolution, Pratt & Whitney accelerated development of its new front-fan JT3D model and began conducting flight tests by fall 1960. P&W also developed a means to convert existing JT3C engines to JT3Ds for much less than the cost of straight replacements. C.R. Smith promptly ordered American's entire 707 and 720 fleet upgraded to the turbofan standard. Meanwhile, orders poured in for new fan-equipped Boeings, and Convair saw its 990 customer base all but disappear.

General Dynamics took a $96.5 million write-off in the third quarter of 1960, for losses on its 880/990 program. Total pre-tax charges against earnings for the entire program stood at $221.5 million.

Flight Testing

The first six 990s off the production line were scheduled to participate in the certification program, including one in static test. As with the 880, Convair did not build a prototype 990.

Following its November 1960 roll-out,

Ship One flew for the first time on January 24, 1961, even as SAS and Swissair announced plans to introduce the 990 over Europe/Far East routes in September. KLM had reportedly selected the airplane and an order was expected in March. In addition, Trans-Canada Airlines showed some interest in the 990 for its medium-range segment needs. Despite these positive indications, Convair had signed up only four customers for a total of 37 airplanes.

Two problem areas that did not surface in the wind tunnel became evident during early flight tests. First, turbulence generated at the junction of the inboard engine pylons and the wing leading edge carried back to the tail and decreased elevator effectiveness. To fix it, electrically operated Krueger-type flaps had to be added in the wing leading edge between the inboard pylons and fuselage. A more serious problem lay in outboard engine oscillations; the power plants would swing side-to-side at cruise speeds when the outboard anti-shock body fuel tanks were full. This more serious problem required shortening of the outboard pylons by 28 inches, accomplished by moving the engines rearward 29 inches.

Ship One went into lay-up for six weeks of modifications on March 21, 1961 while Ship Two, having first flown March 30, continued taxi and systems tests. It was estimated that the changes

First flight: January 24, 1961.   *(General Dynamics)*

Convair 990 Fuel Configurations			
Model	30-5	30-6	30-8
Fuel Tank Capacity (U.S. gallons)			
Wing	10,904	10,904	10,904
Center section	3,125	3,125	3,198
Anti-shock bodies	1,144	1,606	1,606
Total fuel capacity			
U.S. gallons	15,173	15,635	15,708
Pounds	101,659	104,755	105,244

Original customer aircraft deliveries:

30-5: American Airlines, APSA (msn 02/22)
30-6: Swissair, APSA (msn 05)
30-8: Garuda*, Varig, NASA* (msn 01)
* *Built as 30-5 models, fuel configuration upgraded to 30-8.*

would delay FAA certification six months, from June to December. Swissair accepted an offer of two leased 880Ms to fill in until its Coronado fleet began arriving.

In an April 25, 1961 press release announcing the interim 880 plan, Convair stated: "Delay of 990 Coronado deliveries has resulted from a decision to incorporate improvements made on the basis of experience gained in the first stage of the test program."

By month's end, Ship One was back in the air and had successfully flown at Mach .91 without recurrence of the engine pod oscillations. Later, Mach .97 tests were conducted to confirm effectiveness of the fixes. But as flight testing moved into the summer of 1961, Convair engineers knew they were still not out of the woods.

Maximum cruising speeds only came at the cost of excessive fuel burn. Drag problems surfaced around the thrust reverser area and along the wing leading edge. The company acknowledged in August that further financial losses could be expected.

Back To The Bargaining Table

It became clear that the 990 would not live up to its promised performance, particularly in the

areas of speed and range. Even at a reduced speed of 584 mph, coast-to-coast flights were in doubt. More modifications would be expensive and further delay deliveries.

As research continued at Cornell University's Aeronautical Laboratory, Convair went back to American Airlines and offered the option of taking the airplanes unmodified or waiting for new fixes to be completed. American could have canceled its order completely, which would certainly have resulted in the collapse of the entire 990 program, although that might have been the least expensive solution for General Dynamics.

Had other jet transports been available for delivery, American would probably have abandoned its order. Instead, the airline's executives took a deep breath and signed a new agreement on September 21, 1961. The contract was reduced from 25 to 20 units. Fifteen unmodified airplanes, discounted $300,000 each and conditionally accepted, would be in American's hands no later than June 30, 1962 (The per plane price for American would eventually drop to just over $3 million.) In exchange Convair, by February 1963, would develop a fix to attain a maximum cruise speed of 620 mph, still short of originally promised 635 mph. If that requirement could not be attained, the contract would then be considered void, allowing American to return the planes and walk away from the deal.

However, should the original performance guarantees be met, American would then take the last five 990s, for a total of 20. Convair accepted responsibility for American's engine lease agreement with General Electric, and progress payments on the airplanes would be held back by the airline until modifications were realized. In effect, the airline was loaned its 990s during the interim. Delivery of the first two airplanes, for training purposes, was set for December, with service to begin in February 1962. The unmodified speed, guaranteed at 584 mph, would allow American to operate 990s on the same time schedules as its Boeing jets. And if Convair could boost the speed to 620 mph, its claim of "fastest jet transport" would still be valid.

Meanwhile, negotiations commenced with other 990 customers. Swissair agreed to take all seven of its airplanes unmodified, under terms similar to the American agreement. SAS, under a severe financial strain, was already planning to cut back schedules for the 1962 summer season, and eventually canceled its two-plane order, while retaining a separate agreement to lease a pair of 990s from Swissair.

VARIG was not as easy to please, and refused to accept its three-plane order unless the original performance guarantees were met.

The Fix

Once the original elevator and oscillation problems were fixed, Convair needed only to locate and streamline areas of excessive drag on the 990. Three locations were identified for modifications.

The wing leading edge outboard of the inboard pylons had been "drooped" downward to permit slats. Flight testing showed that air flow separation occurred just aft of the slats on the wing underside at low angles of attack, causing additional drag. New wing leading edges were fitted and Krueger flaps, already installed between the inboard pylons and fuselage, replaced the slats between the inboard pylons and wing tips.

The area around the engine thrust reversers was found to be a major drag producer, caused by

990/990A Comparisons

American Airlines Model 30-5

	990	990A
Max. ramp (taxi) weight	240,000 lbs.	247,000 lbs.
Max. gross takeoff weight	239,200 lbs.	246,200 lbs.
Max. landing weight	180,000 lbs.	202,000 lbs.
Max. zero fuel weight	154,000 lbs.	160,000 lbs.
Fuel cap. (US gal.)	15,173	15,173
Normal cruise altitude	35,000 ft.	35,000 ft.
Service ceiling	41,000 ft.	41,000 ft.
Absolute range (still air)	2,970 mi.	3,200 mi.
Engine thrust (sea level)		
CJ-805-23	15,850 lbs.	15,850 lbs.
Maximum cruise speed	595 mph	621 mph

Swissair Model 30-6

	990	990A
Max ramp (taxi) weight	245,000 lbs.	255,000 lbs.
Max. gross takeoff weight	244,200 lbs.	253,000 lbs.
Max. landing weight	180,000 lbs.	202,000 lbs.
Max zero fuel weight	154,000 lbs.	160,000 lbs.
Fuel cap. (US gal.)	15,635	15,635
Normal cruise altitude	35,000 ft.	35,000 ft.
Service ceiling	41,000 ft.	41,000 ft.
Maximum range (full payload)	3,125 mi.	3,595 mi.
Engine thrust (sea level)		
CJ-805-23B	16,050 lbs.	16,050 lbs.
Maximum cruise speed	595 mph	621 mph

the reverser blocker door and sharp change in angle caused by the rear "boat tail" shape. The problem was overcome by altering the aft portions of the pods and covering the blocker doors. A sleeve was installed, extending 7 feet aft of the reverser assembly. It resulted in a lengthened pod with greatly reduced drag. Small suck-in doors were installed in the modified aft section for better performance at takeoff power settings. This modification required design changes in the thrust reversers as well. Testing showed that an inboard protrusion and terminal fairing or "spat," when added to the reverser cowl, would further streamline the assembly. However, this option was adopted only by American Airlines. A crimp in the outboard pylons, that came about as a result of earlier modifications, was straightened during the nacelle work.

Finally, minor drag effects were discovered where the wing joined the fuselage. Convair decided to replace the fillets in this area, and installed considerably larger examples, providing a more gradual junction with the fuselage. The different shape required new frames and refitting of skin.

These changes and other improvements not related to drag problems brought about the 990A configuration. By the time the modification plan was finalized, only six airplanes could actually be built as A models, so it was decided to obtain two type certificates; one for the original design with the outboard pylon and inboard Krueger flap modifications, then another for the 990A.

Airline Deliveries

Both the 990 and 990A were certified under different model designations. The overseas models produced for Swissair and VARIG, also referred to as the Coronado by Swissair, came with slightly more powerful CJ-805-23B engines, had higher maximum operating weights and a could carry a bit more fuel.

The 990 received a U.S. airworthiness certificate on December 18, 1961. American Airlines took delivery of its first example (N5605) on January 7, 1962, and a second on January 12, the same day Swissair received its first Coronado (HB-ICA). VARIG, still in dispute with Convair, would not take its 990s for another year. The overseas version of the 990A received its FAA certification on October 12, 1962, followed by American Airlines' variant in January 1963.

Leftovers

American Airlines eventually accepted the five optioned 990A models, and Swissair bought one

of the two originally earmarked for SAS. VARIG finally took its three airplanes on March 1, 1963; in all, thirty-one 990s were sold to the three original airline customers.

Garuda Indonesian Airways purchased three domestic-configured 990s built for American Airlines, and accepted the first example on October 21. Frederick B. Ayer & Associates bought two 990s used in the flight test program. Neither had received traditional interior furnishings.

Following modifications by the Garret Corporation's AiResearch division, both were leased to Aerolíneas Peruanas (APSA) of Peru.

Convair refurbished and sold Ship One to the National Aeronautics and Space Administration (NASA).

In Retrospect

Even if Convair had met its original goals, the 990s guaranteed speeds would only have been possible at 21,500 feet. Certainly no airline would routinely operate at this altitude except over the shortest routes. Fuel consumption would be nearly double that at economical flight levels, for the sake of an additional 18 knots. American Airlines' blue streak transcons would be pitting speed against fuel capacity. The airplane could have barely made the flight nonstop at Mach .91 under the best conditions. Swissair, attracted to the type by its range rather than speed, found the 990 well suited at high-performance cruise.

When the books were finally closed on the program, General Dynamics had written off $425 million building its 880 and 990 jets. This translated into an average of $4.16 million per airplane, more than most of them sold for. It was, at the time, the largest financial loss by a surviving U.S. corporation.

Chapter Two
CONVAIR 990 INITIAL OPERATORS

Swissair's first Coronado (msn 7) carried a United States registration for pre-delivery test flights.
(General Dynamics)

Swiss Air Transport Co., Ltd. (Swissair)

Swissair originally planned to operate its 990 fleet from Switzerland to the Middle and Far East and to South America, beginning in summer 1961. In addition, two airplanes were to be initially leased to SAS over a four-year period to supplement a pair being purchased directly from Convair by the Scandinavian carrier.

The first aircraft, which were given the name "Coronado" by Swissair, would fly in September 1960 and be part of the flight test program.

When delivery delays were announced, Swissair was more concerned about the Coronado's range performance, needed for the Dakar-Rio de Janeiro trans-Atlantic segment. It reached an agreement similar to that of American Airlines, and accepted

Swissair	
MSN	Reg.
07	HB-ICA
11	HB-ICB
12	HB-ICC
15	HB-ICD
14	HB-ICE
06	HB-ICF
08	HB-ICG
17	HB-ICH

three unmodified examples in January 1962, ten months behind schedule. A fourth 990 arrived at Zürich on February 3, two days before shake-down flights commenced to nearby destinations, including Vienna and London.

A Coronado flew to South America on February 24 and, although one also operated an equipment substitution flight on March 7, the official 990 inaugural departed on the Far East service from Zürich March 9, calling on Cairo, Karachi, Calcutta, Bangkok, Hong Kong, and Tokyo. Either way, Swissair won the distinction of being first to place the type into service. This introduction ended 880 operations at Swissair and the two leased airplanes were returned to Convair.

The Coronados were first configured with 16 first- and 84 economy-class seats, and later modified to accommodate a 14-102 layout.

"A" model upgrades visible on HB-ICA include engine pod extensions and an enlarged wing fillet.
(N. Williams via Terry Waddington)

Swissair reached an agreement on the A model modification program similar to that of American Airlines. Originally, the first three aircraft were to be delivered unmodified, with the last four upgraded prior to delivery, but Swissair later chose to do all the work at Zürich. Once in service, the 990As were found to be fully compliant with performance guarantees, including the maximum range figure which, with a full load, increased from 3,125 to 3,595 miles. All seven aircraft were modified by early 1964.

The 990 fleet eventually operated to nearly all of Swissair's destinations in Europe, the Middle and Far East, and South America plus West Africa, while completing flights for Ghana Airways and Air Afrique. Short-term leases were also completed with Air Ceylon and El Al.

Swiss charter airline Balair leased HB-ICH (msn 17) from 1968, for a variety of missions, including a trans-Atlantic round-trip to Puerto Rico. El Al sub-leased the aircraft using Balair crews, for services between Tel Aviv and London, Brussels, Paris, Rome, and Athens. It also was reportedly sub-leased that year to Air Ceylon. Balair used a 136-seat economy layout during the lease which lasted into 1971.

June 2, 1975: HB-ICC journeys across Lake Lucerne en route to the Swiss Transport Museum. (Swissair)

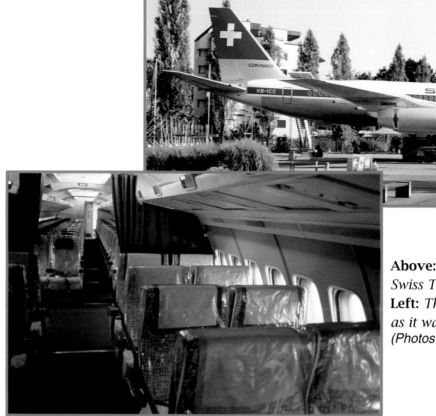

Above: *Swissair's 990A* St. Gallen *at the Swiss Transport Museum.*
Left: *The interior of* St. Gallen *appears just as it was when in airline service.*
(Photos by Robert Farrugia)

Gradually replaced on intercontinental routes by DC-8 and DC-10 equipment, the Swissair Coronado fleet was relegated to short-haul work. With new McDonnell Douglas DC-9-51 twin-jets scheduled to arrive in the following spring, a gradual phase-out of the Coronado fleet commenced in late 1974, and all seven examples were withdrawn by mid-January 1975 after 13 years of service. The final scheduled pattern was a round-trip between Zürich and Nice on January 7, although records indicate the last actual flight occurred on January 16, probably on an equipment substitution or extra section basis.

Four 990s were sold to charter operator Spantax while two others succumbed to the scrapper's guillotine. The remaining airplane — HB-ICC, named *St. Gallen* — flew for the last time on March 20, 1975, to a military airport at Alpnach, Switzerland. On June 2 it was floated on a specially built barge across Lake Lucerne to the Swiss Transport Museum and placed outside on permanent display. *St. Gallen* had gained distinction in 1969 when it carried Pope Paul IV on his visit to Geneva. The papal seal worn on the special flight was reapplied, just ahead of the forward passenger door. A Swissair representative remains at the museum to look after its star attraction, which was recently given a fresh coat of paint.

American Airlines, Inc.

American Airlines took delivery of its first 990 (N5605) on January 7, 1962 for crew training and route proving flights. Four airplanes were on hand by the time service was inaugurated on March 18, with two daily round-trips between New York-Idlewild and Chicago-O'Hare, over a year after its first turbofan-powered 707 and 720 flights began.

American's original all-first-class layout would have provided 92 seats, plus a six-seat lounge, but that plan was long forgotten when 990s were deployed over medium-haul routes. A 42 first-class and 57 coach seat configuration was adopted, with a four-place lounge at the front of first-class, opposite the galley. First-class was later reduced to 34 seats, increasing coach to 67.

Above: *An unmodified American 990 on display at a Miramar Naval Air Station open house.* *(Nicholas A. Veronico collection)*

Below: *N5603 came to American already in the 990A configuration. This updated color scheme was applied in 1964.* *(Peter W. Black collection)*

American		
MSN	Fleet #	Reg.
33	601	N5601*
34	602	N5602*
35	603	N5603*
36	604	N5604*
09	605	N5605
10	606	N5606
16	607	N5607
18	608	N5608
21	609	N5609
22	610	N5610
23	611	N5611
24	612	N5612
25	613	N5613
26	614	N5614
27	615	N5615
28	616	N5616
29	617	N5617
30	618	N5618
31	619	N5619
32	620	N5620*
* Delivered as 990A		

The last of American's 15-plane order was received on June 29, 1962, allowing rapid expansion of service for the summer season.

With double-digit growth in passenger traffic, American decided to accept the last five Convairs, for delivery in the first quarter of 1963. Although the revised contract originally called for A model upgrades to be completed by Convair at San Diego, the airline elected to do the modifications at its Tulsa, Oklahoma maintenance base and be reimbursed by the manufacturer. All were flying as 990As by the end of 1964. By this time, the airline had adopted a new color scheme, featuring a circle logo on the tail, modified "lightning bolt" fuselage cheatline and stylized titles. It first appeared on Boeing 727s which began arriving several months earlier.

In 1965, a decision was made to begin phasing out the Convairs, well before the fleet approached mid-life status. N5619 was the first to depart, on October 19, sold to Lebanese International Airways. A second example was handed over to the same carrier three months later.

Following a one-year hiatus, eight Convairs were sold off in 1967. American retired the type from service at the end of October 1968, disposing of four more that year, and the remaining five in 1969. Among the last scheduled segments was a 2,143-mile New York-Phoenix nonstop, which turned out to be the longest regularly flown by an American 990. Its original coast-to-coast mission never came to fruition.

Sales became complicated in 1968 when American repossessed three 990s from Internord of Sweden. One of these ships, plus five more, were sold to Middle East Airlines of Lebanon, then re-acquired in exchange for used Boeing 720Bs. Upon return, some of the ships were given registrations originally assigned to other 990s, causing confusion. For example, N5604 (msn 36) received

N5612 upon its repossession from Internord, a number previously worn by msn 24. It appears that none of the returned airplanes were reactivated prior to resale, including msn 25, which came back from both Internord and MEA, claiming no less than three different tail numbers! The last example to depart for good was msn 25, delivered to Spantax on May 18, 1972.

Launch customer American Airlines stood by its decision to acquire the 990, but only operated the type for seven years.

American's 990 first-class lounge.
(Scott Haskin collection)

Scandinavian Airlines System
Thai International Airways

As previously mentioned, SAS originally ordered two Convair 990s, and later canceled the order more out of economic necessity than dissatisfaction with the airplane. But it did complete a four year lease of two examples from Swissair as planned. SAS received both directly from Convair.

SE-DAY (msn 08) was delivered on February 23, 1962 in full SAS colors, named *Adils Viking,* and

In the dual colors of SAS and Thai, SE-DAY (msn 8) pauses at Zürich-Kloten. (Peter Keating)

configured for 42 first-class and 57 coach passengers. It was placed into service between Copenhagen and Tokyo with intermediate stops.

The second aircraft — SE-DAZ, *Ring Viking* — arrived April 10, 1962. Both examples were operated on sub-lease agreements with Thai Airways International (in which SAS had a financial stake), and wore basic SAS colors with dual titles above the window line. The inaugural Thai flight occurred on May 18, 1962. *Ring Viking* continued with Thai until the end of 1963, renamed *Srisuriyothai,* and was registered HS-TGE during the lease period. Upon returning to SAS, the aircraft was assigned to South Atlantic routes.

Both Coronados were handed back to Swissair on February 1, 1966.

Leased from Swissair, the first 990 for SAS climbs out of San Diego's Lindbergh Field.
(General Dynamics)

SAS	
MSN	Registration
06	LN-LMA*
08	SE-DAY
14	SE-DAZ*
17	SE-DAZ/HS-TGE
* order canceled	

Viação Aérea Rio-Grandense, S.A. (VARIG)

Msn 13 PP-VJE, msn 19 PP-VJF, msn 20 PP-VJG

Wearing original colors, Varig's PP-VJF (msn 19) leaves San Diego already modified to the A configuration. (General Dynamics)

As with Swissair, Viação Aérea Rio-Grandense, S.A., doing business as VARIG, was more concerned with performance than speed when it came to accepting its three 990s. But unlike Swissair and American, the carrier refused to accept the airplanes unmodified, despite attempts by Convair to force the sale at the beginning of 1962.

Having taken over responsibility for the contract when it absorbed REAL-Aerovías of Brazil, VARIG was not that anxious to receive 990s, and probably would have canceled the order, were it not for $5 million in progress payments already handed over to the manufacturer.

The stalemate was broken a year later, following demonstration flights on VARIG's routes, and all three 990s were handed over on March 1, 1963. Service commenced between Los Angeles and Porto Alegre, Brazil via Mexico City, Bogotá, Lima, Rio de Janeiro, and São Paulo. Flights to Miami were added later.

Originally flying Conway-powered Boeing 707s, VARIG became one of the few airlines to operate the Convair 990, Boeing 707 and Douglas DC-8, when it took over the European routes of defunct Panair do Brasil in 1965. More 707s were ordered for expansion and to standardize on single long-haul jet type. As the Boeing deliveries continued, one Convair, PP-VJE, was sold to Alaska Airlines, in 1967. The other two were retained until 1971, then purchased by Modern Air Transport, closing out eight years of 990 service.

Garuda Indonesian Airways

Msn 03 PK-GJA, msn 04 PK-GJB, msn 37 PK-GJC

Garuda supplemented its Lockheed 188 Electras with three 990A domestic models originally built for American Airlines and upgraded from 30-5 to 30-8 engine and fuel capacity standards. All were received between September 1963 and January 1964. Early flights were over the company's Emerald Service routes from Jakarta to Hong Kong and Tokyo via Bangkok and Manila.

Named Pajajaran, *Garuda's first 990 is seen on a station stop at Hong Kong.* (Peter Keating)

Australian operations were later added plus European flights to Rome and Amsterdam via Bombay and Cairo.

Leased DC-8 equipment began replacing 990s on the European service in 1968. One of the Convairs was destroyed in a takeoff accident that year, and the remaining two were withdrawn from service by 1972 as additional Douglas jets came on-line.

Aerolíneas Peruanas, S.A. (APSA)

Msn 05 OB-OAG/OB-R-728, msn 02 OB-R-765, msn 24 OB-R-925

APSA leased a single 990 from Frederick B. Ayer & Associates with a purchase option and introduced jet service December 23, 1963 on a route from Miami — where its mainly American crews were domiciled — to Bogatá, Lima, and Buenos Aires. Miami-Rio de Janeiro flights commenced November 7, 1964 with a single stop at Lima. Departure and arrival times in Florida were scheduled for convenient connections with Northeast Airlines flights to New York via Convair 880s. São Paulo and Panama service was added later, in addition to La Paz, Asunción, and Montevideo.

Configured for 119 passengers, the cabin was fitted with five-across seating and a forward

APSA's OB-R-728 (msn 5) rolls out after landing at Los Angeles International. (Terry Waddington)

lounge plus attractive Peruvian murals on the cabin divider walls.

A second 990, also acquired from F.B. Ayer, began flying with APSA March 1, 1965, allowing new service from Lima to Mexico City via Guayaquil, a route which was extended to Los Angeles the following year.

Options were exercised to purchase the two Convairs, plus one additional example, returned to F.B. Ayer by Northeast Airlines. It was leased in June 1968 as APSA continued its expansion. European service commenced in 1969 but with a DC-8 leased from Iberia.

Unfortunately, APSA over-expanded and ran deeply into debt. The airline suddenly shut down on May 3, 1971, after its three Convairs were repossessed. Two would never fly passenger flights again.

A dramatic shot of OB-R-965 (msn 24) at Mexico City in September 1968 (Phil Glatt collection)

National Aeronautics & Space Administration (NASA)

NASA leased, then purchased, for $2.5 million, 990 Ship One from Convair, to use as a research aircraft. Prior to delivery, the airplane was upgraded with CJ805-23B engines and additional fuel capacity. Thirteen viewing ports were installed along the upper fuselage. Equipped with special optical glass covers, the windows were used for scientific observations. Electronic refinements and added instrumentation were also incorporated.

Named *Galileo,* the unique 990 flew a variety of missions from the Ames Research Center at Moffett Field in Sunnyvale, California. The airplane was fitted with special laboratory-like electrical power supplies, and contained a permanently installed data recording and processing system, valued at $1 million. It could accommodate 30 research scientists, and was shared by several departments within NASA. Heavy maintenance was done on a contract basis by American Jet Industries at Van Nuys, California, the same company that purchased TWA's 880s in 1978.

Galileo completed several special solar eclipse observation flights, including one in May 1965 which operated from Hilo, Hawaii. With its high approach and landing speeds, the 990 was able to perform simulated landings for the upcoming space shuttle program. It completed 14 major astronomical, meteorological, and atmospheric expeditions prior to being tragically lost on April 12, 1973 in a mid-air collision; all aboard were killed.

California Airmotive acquired two ex-Garuda aircraft in June 1973 for the purpose of providing NASA with a replacement aircraft and probably intended to use the second example as a spares source. Both were provided maintenance at Hong Kong and departed for the United States. However, one airplane (msn 4) suffered major damage in a landing accident at Guam where a fuel stop had

Above: Galileo II at the Paris Air Show.
(Michel Gilliand/Jon Proctor collection)

Top: 990 Ship One leaves San Diego for a new career with NASA.
(General Dynamics)

NASA	
MSN	**Registration**
29	N710NA, N713NA, N810NA
01	N711NA
37	N712NA

NASA's Landing Systems Research Aircraft (LSRA) at the Dryden Flight Research Center, Edwards, California.
(NASA)

been scheduled. Major components were salvaged for spare parts and the remains broken up.

The second 990 (msn 37) became N711NA, appropriately christened *Galileo II.* It received treatment similar to that given the original Galileo, and served NASA for 12 years. Incredibly, this airplane was also lost, after an aborted takeoff at March Air Force Base, California on July 17, 1985.

NASA had purchased yet another 990 in 1975. Formerly with American Airlines and then Modern Air Transport, the plane and a spare engine were

acquired for $250,000. After minimal upgrades msn 29 was used, along with *Galileo II,* for medium-atmospheric research in 1975, and then stored at Marana, Arizona. The N713NA registration was changed in 1978 — perhaps out of superstition — to N710NA. It was reactivated in 1980 for a three-year military support operation, based at Ames, then returned to hibernate at Marana.

In 1988, a proposal was made to heavily modify it for use as a Landing Systems Research Aircraft (LSRA), in support of the Space Shuttle program. The orbiters, which land without engine power, could not be used to verify landing systems, hence the need for a test vehicle. In addition to evaluating new tire compounds and runway surfaces, NASA wanted to verify cross-wind limits and landing speed variations. Such testing was critical to increase the shuttle's ability to routinely land at the Kennedy Space Center (KSC) in Florida instead of Edwards Air Force Base, California, which required a $1 million 747 piggy-back ride back to KSC.

Selected for its rugged structure and availability, N710NA's identity was changed again, this time to

Highly modified LSRA in flight, showing the space shuttle test landing gear installation. Note that the Convair's main wheels are permanently locked down while the nose gear is retractable. Also visible are the nacelle inboard terminal fairing spats adopted during A model conversions on American Airlines 30A-5 examples. Blade radio antenna protrudes from the vertical stabilizer.
(NASA)

Among the last tests was this "roll-on-rims" drill (left) conducted on an Edwards concrete runway that produced dramatic results. Tire failure parameters tests (below) using the dry lake bed were less spectacular. (NASA photos)

N810NA, as it entered an extensive modification program in January 1991 at the agency's Dryden Flight Research Center at Edwards, California. With Convair engineers acting in an advisory role, NASA personnel began the major retrofit necessary to incorporate a shuttle main landing gear assembly between the 990's main gear. This required cutting out a section of the airplane's center keel and replacing it with two auxiliary beams on each side of the fuselage. Three new bulkheads were installed along with heavy metal plating to upgrade structural integrity and protect against damage from tires.

A complete fire suppression system was added, in the form of two 100-gallon water tanks in the forward belly, able to handle any eventuality during the landing tests, conducted at 256 mph (flaps up) to duplicate the orbiter's speed.

The elaborate, hydraulically operated, test gear actuator system fills much of the passenger cabin, along with control systems consoles and operator stations. The conversion added 40,000 pounds to N810NA, which now weighs in at just over 200,000 pounds. Its main landing gear has been bolted in place and can no longer be raised (the nose gear is unaffected), restricting cruising speed to 432 knots, or 496 mph. With the shuttle test gear actuator extension extending into the cabin, pressurization is no longer possible, so the airplane stays below 13,000 feet. A trip from Edwards to Florida requires an en route fuel stop. These speed and altitude restrictions seem rather cruel for an airplane once claimed to be the world's fastest transport, but, considering the alternatives, such humiliations can be endured.

After 155 test flights which stretched over two years, N810NA was parked at Edwards on August 11, 1995. The last flights included some rather spectacular "roll-on-rims" tests, conducted on both concrete runways and Edwards' dry lakebed surfaces to measure performance with the tires deliberately failed. On concrete the result was a fireball which reached from the test landing gear to the window line and beyond the tail.

When justifying the project, NASA estimated that if test data supplied by the LSRA eliminated just one space shuttle transfer between California and Florida, the savings would easily cover the entire program's cost. In the end, crosswind landing limits for the shuttle were increased from 15 to 20 knots.

The venerable 990, felt to be a good source for future High-Speed Civil Transport landing research, remains parked at the Dryden center. Though inactive, this unique test and research vehicle is available for future use in programs with other government agencies. Hopefully it will get plenty of requests.

Chapter Three
CONVAIR 990 SUBSEQUENT OPERATORS

Denver Ports-of-Call

Denver Ports-of-Call (POC) was formed in 1966 as a travel club operating under Federal Air Regulation (FAR) Part 123 rules. Beginning with a Douglas DC-7, the organization upgraded to a DC-7C in 1969 and an Electra in 1972 before purchasing one of the former APSA 990s (msn 24) on October 24, 1973. Six more examples were acquired from Modern Air Transport, with two coming in 1975 and the balance a year later, including a pair used for spare parts which never entered service. The five-plane fleet took club members on extended flights all over the world, and operated segments as long as the 3,365 mile Honolulu-Denver leg.

Denver Ports-of-Call	
MSN	Registration
33	N5601
26	N5614
09	N8160C
19	N8258C
20	N8259C
27	N8356C
24	N8357C

FAR 123 was abolished in 1981, and travel clubs operating aircraft in excess of 25,000 pounds were brought under the new FAR 125, that permitted Ports-of-Call to operate affinity and incentive group charters for other organizations.

Top: *N8259C (msn 20) on approach to Stapleton International Airport, Denver, looking smart in POC's updated livery.* (Peter W. Black)
Above: *N8258C (msn 19) in original Ports-of-Call markings. Note the friendly engine intake covers.*
(Jon Proctor Collection)

Left: *POC's 149-seat cabin interior featured colors popular in the mid-1970s.* **Above:** *One of the two forward lavatories was removed to accommodate an auxiliary galley, bar, and storage area. Visible cords are bar "cobra head" beverage dispensers.*
(both Michael Bolden collection)

This new flexibility prompted the club to begin acquiring more equipment and Boeing 707s were chosen. After withdrawing one 990 a year earlier, a second example was put down in 1981, but the remaining three (msn 20, 24, 27), wearing attractive updated color schemes, soldiered on until the end of December 1984 when new U.S. federal noise regulations forced the Convairs into retirement.

Five-Seven-Charlie

Headed for Ciskei with new titles, Five-Seven-Charlie begins its takeoff roll at Marana. *(Bob Shane)*

After living in retirement at Marana, Arizona, N8357C (msn 24) of Denver Ports-of-Call was refurbished and sent off to the South African Independent State of Ciskei in January 1988, as a U.S. flag carrier. Unable to secure necessary operating permits, the airline flew a single "pre-inaugural" flight to Johannesburg but never began regular service. After being parked at Ostend, Belgium, the airplane was purchased by Greco Air in 1991 and ferried to El Paso, Texas where it remains in storage.

Lebanese International Airways

MSN 31 OD-AEW, 10 OD-AEX

Lebanese International Airways (LIA), faced with jet competition from Middle East Airlines, agreed during the summer of 1965 to purchase two second-hand 990s from American Airlines, and took an option on a third. The first Convair (msn 31) was placed into service December 23, fitted with 14 first- and 107 tourist-class seats. It was scheduled to fly on nearly every sector of LIA's route network. All European services were taken over, with twice-weekly schedules to Milan and Paris, plus a weekly flight to Zürich. Other destinations included Kuwait, Doha, Bombay, and Tehran.

The second 990 joined LIA in February 1966, allowing transition to all-jet service and expansion of flights. Convair service continued through 1967 and into 1968 but heavy competition — chiefly from MEA — took a toll on finances, and the option for a third airplane was not taken up. By summer's end, payments to American Airlines had fallen behind; over $5 million was owed and the 990s could have been repossessed. Instead, American reached an agreement to acquire a 31 percent interest in LIA and provide both technical and managerial assistance.

The airline's tenuous position suddenly became moot on December 28, 1968 when Israeli commandos staged a night helicopter raid on Beirut Airport in retaliation for the destruction of an Israeli plane at Athens a few days earlier. In addition to 12 other aircraft casualties, both 990s were destroyed. LIA was out of business.

Above: *Lebanese International's OD-AEX (msn 10) reflects Arabic fuselage titles. (Barney Deatrick)*
Below: *OD-AEW (msn 31) begins to pull away from the gate at Paris. Both LIA 990s were destroyed during an Israeli commando raid at Beirut on December 28, 1968.   (Terry Waddington Collection)*

Middle East Airlines AirLiban SAL
(MEA)

Having utilized a variety of jetliner equipment in the early and mid-1960s, Middle East Airlines (MEA) took advantage of early deliveries by acquiring on a lease-purchase arrangement, a fleet of six 990s from American Airlines in 1969 for medium- and long-haul operations. All were delivered between June and December, and quickly entered service alongside Boeing 707s, gradually replacing Caravelle and Comet IVC examples.

By the following spring, 990 "Cedar Jets" were flying scheduled services from Beirut to Amman, Ankara, Cairo, Copenhagen, Frankfurt, Geneva, Istanbul, Milan, Paris, Vienna, and Zürich.

Middle East Airlines	
MSN	Registration
18	OD-AFF
30	OD-AFG
25	OD-AFH
35	OD-AFI
33	OD-AFJ
26	OD-AFK

As MEA acquired additional 707 equipment, it made sense to standardize on Boeing jets. American Airlines was beginning to sell off its excess 720B equipment and agreed to take back the six Convairs in partial payment for what eventually grew to include 13 of the short Boeings, followed by four 707-323C aircraft. All six Convairs were returned by February 1972.

MEA operated six former American Airlines 990s for three years before re-equipping with Boeing jets. *(Terry Waddington collection)*

Modern Air Transport

Organized in 1946 as a non-scheduled carrier, Modern Air Transport (MAT) was granted supplemental charter airline status in 1966, with authority to provide air service in the United States and from the U.S. to Canada and Mexico.

During the same year, Gulf American Land Corporation (GAC) bought the airline and used it to fly prospective buyers to the company's land developments in Florida and Arizona. Modern's headquarters were moved to Miami from Trenton, New Jersey, and Gulf American ordered five 990s from American Airlines to replace the airline's con-

glomeration of piston and leased jet equipment. The first Convair (N5607) was delivered on January 4, 1967 and entered service in a 139-seat charter configuration.

The new jet acquisitions overwhelmed the little carrier, and financial losses mounted quickly. After only three Convairs had begun flying, MAT attempted unsuccessfully to cancel the last two deliveries and began laying off employees. A new management team was brought in and concentrated on the newly acquired jet fleet. It sold off all other aircraft and leased out three 990s to Nordair during the 1968 summer season. Following a painful period which included a realignment and more layoffs, Modern Air began to turn the corner toward profitability.

Above: *N5605 (msn 9) poses at Hartford-Springfield in July 1974.*   (Terry Waddington collection)
Opposite Page, Lower: *Modern Air's first color scheme featured "The Silver Palace" titles.*
(Jon Proctor collection)

In addition to Florida and Arizona land charters, it was able to better compete with its Convairs, and even flew twice-weekly trans-Atlantic charters from Montréal.

With the arrival of its fourth and fifth 990s, MAT began operations out of Tegel Airport in what was then West Berlin, enjoying far more liberal inclusive tour regulations than were allowed in the United States. Initially, two Convairs were based at Tegel with a third added for busy summer traffic. From its new German base, Modern branched out to other European destinations and such distant cities as Bangkok and Johannesburg.

A sixth 990, originally flown by VARIG and acquired from Alaska Airlines, joined the fleet the same year, followed by two more examples from American in January 1971, accompanied by AA's remaining spare parts inventory. Finally, Modern purchased VARIG's other two Convairs the following summer, bringing its fleet strength to eight, claimed as "the world's largest Convair 990 jet fleet." (In 1970, the ex-Alaska ship was lost in an accident and N5609 was sold to Spantax.)

Under progressive management, MAT significantly enhanced its 990 fleet. A Miami-based company utilizing an English design produced a comfortable slimmer seat which would allow two more rows without reduction in leg room. The result was a capacity increase of 10 seats, to 149.

Except for major airframe and engine overhauls, all maintenance was performed in-house, most of it at the extensive Miami facility purchased by GAC in 1970 from American Airmotive. MAT mechanics, working with Garrett AiResearch, designed the first ever 990 auxiliary power unit (APU) and ingeniously installed it within the inboard anti-shock body on the starboard wing, utilizing a hollow area aft of the fuel tank. Unfortunately the unit did not live up to expectations; only one installation was completed, and later removed.

As fuel costs rose, Modern gradually reduced

Modern Air's Polar Byrd I *was the first commercial jet to land on the ice runway at McMurdo Sound.*
(Morton S. Beyer collection)

Modern Air	
MSN	Registration
33	N5601
09	N5605
16	N5607
21	N5609
26	N5614
27	N5615
29	N5617
20	N5623
16	N5624
19	N5625

The one and only Busenvogel *flight.*
(Morton S. Beyer collection)

cruising speeds from Mach .85 all the way down to Mach .78, with major economic improvements and a range increase exceeding 20 percent. One Modern Air flight, with a full load of passengers, completed a 4,319-mile Philadelphia-to-Vienna segment.

As the flight was about to depart, an American Airlines pilot reportedly came aboard to admire the aircraft, which he had flown before its sale to MAT. "Where are you headed for?" he asked the captain. "Vienna," came the reply. "Oh? Where are you stopping for fuel?" When told "We're not," he remarked, "I couldn't even get one of these across the country nonstop, let alone the Atlantic Ocean!"

Among MAT's other Convair accomplishments were two trans-polar round-the-world luxury charter flights. *Polar Byrd I* in 1968 had the distinction of being the first commercial jet to land on the ice runway at McMurdo Sound, Antarctica, and also became the first U.S. charter flight to visit the Soviet Union, during a hastily planned Moscow side trip. Unfortunately, Russian ground power unit (GPU) fittings did not match the Convair's air intake valve, and the return departure was delayed three days until a Modern Air GPU could be brought in from West Berlin.

A similar pole-to-pole charter was repeated in 1970. However, these epic journeys were probably overshadowed in the press by a one-day junket from West Berlin to Paris, also in 1970. N5615,

used for both polar charters, gained a place in aviation folklore by operating a special Father's Day trip, also billed as a "Get Away From Mama Flight." In addition to the regular cabin crew, German showgirls greeted the 110 passengers and served champagne in rather flimsy outfits with transparent bodices. Sadly, the unique *Busenvogel* (Bosombird) flight, which drew world-wide press coverage, was not repeated.

In 1971 a change in the GAC board of directors prompted the company to suddenly move all of its flights to West Berlin, based on only marginal stateside losses. Because this served to push European operations into the red, limited stateside operations were reinstated the following year. When parent GAC filed for reorganization under bankruptcy rules, the "umbilical cord" was cut, and, with the land package tour business lost, Modern Air never fully recovered. German operations were suspended at the end of the 1974 season and three 990s were sold. The situation only worsened in 1975 as more aircraft were parked and disposed of. The pilots walked out September 1 in a contract dispute, leaving two aircraft at New York-JFK and one at Chicago-O'Hare. GAC Corp. publicly announced it could invest no further in the airline, and, on October 6, 1975, the Civil Aeronautics Board permanently grounded Modern Air Transport and its 990s by revoking the company's operating certificate.

EC-CNF can be recognized as an ex-Swissair ship from the CORONADO titles on its tail.

(Terry Waddington)

Spantax, S.A.

The name Spantax is actually an anagram, reflecting the airlines' origin as a Spanish air taxi service formed in 1959. A year later it began carrying tourists within the Canary Islands and quickly grew to become a major air charter business, operating mainly in the Inclusive Tour (IT) arena between major European cities and Spanish resorts in the Canary and Balearic Islands.

In 1967 Spantax purchased two 990s from American Airlines, placing the first (EC-BJC) into service on April 1 between Palma and Madrid. Rodolfo Bay, the airline's co-founder and president, became perhaps the world's greatest 990 supporter. Captain Rudi, as he was affectionately known, praised the airplane, saying, "Once you fly a Coronado, you don't want to fly anything else. The aircraft is fast, has a very strong structure, admittedly is a bit quick over the threshold, but will stop on any runway as the reverse thrust is available promptly." Bay is generally credited with first having called the 990 "the Maserati of the air,"

and for years was hailed as "King of the Coronados!"

Spantax bought eight more ex-American Airlines Convairs between 1968 and 1972, one via Modern Air Transport. Another four came from Swissair in 1975, and could be identified by Coronado titles on the tail, plus EC registrations which began with C instead of B. The airline accumulated a 990 fleet second in size only to American Airlines, and averaged 2,300 flying hours annually per airplane.

As with Modern Air, Spantax increased its 990 seating capacity to 149, buying modification kits consisting of tubing and skeleton frames, then

Wearing an interim color scheme with original fuselage stripes and new tail markings and titles, EC-BQA is seen two months prior to retirement.

(Terry Waddington)

75

EC-BZO was the last operational Spantax 990, and sports the airline's final
livery. *(Phil Brooks Collection)*

installing the upholstery and seat hardware at its Palma maintenance base. The company also reduced cruising speeds in steps — from Mach .86 to Mach .80 — in order to compensate for increased fuel prices. In 1975 work began to modify the Spantax CJ-805-23 engines with GE-designed smokeless combustion chambers, substantially reducing the Convair's signature exhaust trail, and unexpectedly improving fuel burn by 1 percent.

As operating costs continued to grow, the 990 fleet was gradually withdrawn from service, starting in March 1981. Some of the Convairs were temporarily stored, then returned to flight status. It appears that -BZO and -BQQ were the last two operational aircraft, and the only ones fully painted in the company's updated color scheme. EC-BZO reportedly operated the final 990 service for Spantax in March 1987. Eight aircraft were scrapped at Palma in 1991 and two in 1993.

By the end of 1995, EC-BQQ had been reduced to a hulk, with its outer wings removed, along with most usable parts, but -BZO remains at Palma in good condition. Plans for its preservation in a Madrid museum apparently have not yet come to fruition.

Lineas Aéreas De España, S.A. (Iberia)

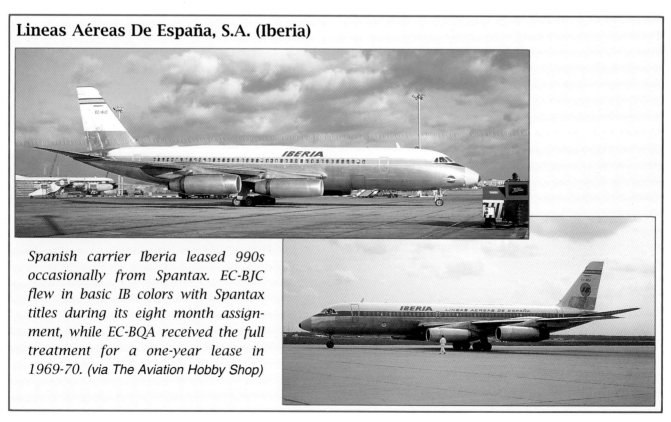

Spanish carrier Iberia leased 990s occasionally from Spantax. EC-BJC flew in basic IB colors with Spantax titles during its eight month assignment, while EC-BQA received the full treatment for a one-year lease in 1969-70. *(via The Aviation Hobby Shop)*

Chapter Four
990 Other Operators

Modern Air wet-leased N5605 (msn 9) to Air France in 1967 for use on the London-Paris run.
(Peter W. Black collection)

The only airline to actually own both 880 and 990 equipment, Alaska Airlines purchased one of each. N987AS was acquired in May 1967 and flew the company's main jet routes until leased to AREA of Ecuador in March 1968. It was eventually sold to Modern Air.
(Peter W. Black collection)

Aerovías Ecuatorianas C Ltda. (AREA) of Ecuador leased a 990 from Alaska Airlines in 1968, for use on its route from Guayaquil to La Paz-Asunción and terminating in Montevideo. The tail later was adorned with an "A."
(Terry Waddington collection)

HB-ICA (msn 7) wore stickers while operating short-term lease flights for Air Afrique.
(Aviation Photo News)

HB-ICH (msn 17) was converted to an all-economy layout in spring 1974 and leased to Balair, which in turn sub-leased it to El Al for a few weeks to fly routes between Tel Aviv and Paris, Brussels, and Zürich.
(Barney Deatrick)

Ghana Airways leased this Swissair Coronado (msn 14) in 1964 for twice-weekly service between London and Accra.
(Peter Keating)

Consolidated Components, Inc., doing business as Galaxy Airlines, operated a single 990 (msn 16) during 1984-85, principally on gambling junkets between Ft. Lauderdale, Florida, and Freeport, Bahamas, although it is known to have made at least one trip to Reno, Nevada, via Buffalo, New York. Galaxy titles were applied, but the 990 was operating under Part 125 (rather than Part 121) of U.S. Federal Air Regulations, which allowed no visual advertising of any kind, forcing removal of the name. The aircraft remained parked at Ft. Lauderdale and, in 1990 was registered to Christ Is The Answer, of El Paso, Texas. Appropriate titles were added, but plans for missionary flights were not fulfilled, and the plane was finally scrapped on the spot in 1991. (Phil Glatt-top) (Phil Brooks-lower)

Formed on November 30, 1965 by the merger of Osterman Air Charter of Sweden and Aero-Nord of Denmark, charter operator Internord operated DC-7 and DC-7B equipment until acquiring three 990s (msn 25/34/36) from American Airlines. Two were delivered in 1967, and the third in 1968. OY-ANI oper-

ated the first service on June 28, 1967. Inclusive tours were flown mainly from points in Sweden and Denmark to the Mediterranean and Canary Islands. The carrier was not financially successful, and ceased operations October 30, 1968. All three 990s were repossessed by American and returned to the U.S. via Goose Bay, Labrador. (Terry Waddington)

Detroit-based Nomads travel club celebrated its 10th anniversary in 1975 by acquiring a 990 from Modern Air Transport. The Convair flew its first passenger-carrying trip to the Bahamas. While with Nomads, N990E (msn 16) completed two round-the-world trips, plus excursions to other overseas destinations. With the acquisition of a Boeing 727 in 1981, the 990 was retired and later sold.   (ATP/Airliners America)

Nordair of Canada leased three 990s from Modern Air in 1968 — including N5615 (msn 27) — for Caribbean and European charter flights.
(Terry Waddington)

Northeast Airlines' sole 990, *Flagship Rita*, was leased From F.B. Ayer from January 1967 for New York-Miami service, and returned in April of the following year.
(Peter W. Black)

N5601 (msn 33), a POC spare parts airplane (seen above), became The Convair Restaurant at Tri-County Airport, Erie, Colorado. The eatery ceased operations in 1991.

(Above: John Whitehead)
(Left: Robert P. Austin)

EPILOGUE

Convair engineers made several follow-up design proposals to either succeed or supplement the 880 and 990 programs.

In 1960, the Model 60 was considered as a replacement for the Convair twins. Utilizing two wing-mounted turbofan engines, it would have accommodated 68-85 passengers, with a 1,600 mile range. When little interest was generated by this design, Convair produced plans for the smaller Model 38. The 48-seat example featured tail-mounted Rolls Royce RB-195 bypass engines. Application for type certification was made in August 1963, with a proposed November 1965 first flight date. Once again the program was canceled for lack of interested buyers. As time began to run out, the employees at San Diego even proposed a plan to convert 880 Ship One to a twin-engine prototype, working without pay. Sadly, the tooling and construction jigs were dismantled, and the offer was ignored. Convair was out of the passenger airliner business.

Years later, a plan to retrofit the 880 with either de-rated General Electric CF6-6 or CFM56 engines was considered; Gulfstream American's fleet had been targeted for conversion. Not surprisingly, this 1980 idea did not become reality although engineering work on it continued through late 1984. With only a handful of aircraft to retrofit, design costs could not be spread out sufficiently to justify such an expenditure.

With the completion of 990 msn 37 in the early 1960s, activity at the San Diego plant became limited to component production and assembly projects. Having lost its critical mass, Convair began moving its remaining programs to General Dynamics. Buildings 5 and 51 were refurbished, however, and used until 1994 for the secret full-scale development of the U.S. Air Force AGM-129A advanced cruise missile. Otherwise, the Lindbergh Field facility was shut down.

A startling development occurred when the company's Convair Service Center division reached an agreement with Spantax to convert that airline's 990s to six-across seating for European inclusive tour charters. The extensive modifications would have been carried out at San Diego and airline officials signed a contract just as a greater opportunity presented itself.

Convair agreed to design and build DC-10 fuselage sections for McDonnell Douglas and it needed the factory space. An alternate site in Arizona was selected for the 990 work, but General Dynamics decided against it and canceled the project, which had also stirred interest at Modern Air Transport. The six-abreast arrangement that jinxed Convair's jets from early on nearly came to fruition.

The DC-10 program was succeeded by that of the MD-11, launched in the mid-1980s, but orders were not sufficient to operate the huge San Diego facility on a profitable basis. In 1994 Convair announced it would terminate the contract with McDonnell Douglas by the end of 1995.

As the last fuselage barrel moved down the assembly line, idled stations behind it were dismantled and employees laid off. In November, an auctioneer was brought in to sell off equipment to the highest bidders. More than 1,000 buyers, including other aircraft manufacturers, quickly snapped up the machinery.

In January 1996 Convair shut down for good. The 95-acre site its plant occupies is owned by the Port of San Diego, which announced demolition plans. At the time of this writing, a group of concerned San Diegans has proposed converting the facility into a transportation museum, but the city, in danger of losing its symphony orchestra to budgetary constraints, is reluctant to undertake such a project. It remains to be seen whether or not the last visible signs of a proud company with ties back to 1908 will survive.

PART III

Safety

Ship One made an unplanned appearance at Edwards Air Force Base with its rudder missing and vertical stabilizer nearly torn away following flutter tests over the Pacific. Note the unusual engine nacelle logo symbols.   (Edwards Air Force Base Archives)

The 880

The 880 attained a good safety record in passenger service, but suffered numerous training mishaps, and several accidents occurred after the airplanes were converted to freighter configurations. At least 15 hull loses were recorded, including several which were repairable but written off due to economic considerations.

The first airplane built nearly became a statistic during the certification program, over a year before the type entered scheduled service. On March 25, 1959, flight tests with N801TW were being conducted over the Pacific Ocean when most of the rudder and about half of the vertical stabilizer were torn from the airplane. With the test engineers in parachutes and ready to bail out, chief test pilot Don Germeraad found he could maintain control with differential engine thrust. Following a denied request to land at Lindbergh Field he was able to accomplish a precautionary landing at Edwards Air Force Base, California.

Wind tunnel testing had led to the installation of three hydraulic dampers on the rudder and elevators to counteract any fluttering tendencies. Convair engineers decided to test the rudder with one damper removed. The results were dramatic; severe buffeting led to structural failure. Three dampers became standard on production models. N801TW was repaired and back in the test program less than two weeks after the incident.

Engine-out Training Accidents

The 880 was involved in an inordinate number of training accidents involving engine-out drills. Describing the root cause of these mishaps requires a somewhat technical explanation of the airplane's aerodynamic characteristics.

With the advent of jet transports, pilots were taught about the increased urgency of prompt rudder corrections when encountering an engine failure on takeoff to counteract the resulting yaw towards the dead power plant. By its design, the 880 was especially susceptible to this tendency. Its engines were widely spaced on the wings, and a loss of power from an outboard example caused an asymmetrical thrust problem which could quickly send the airplane off the side of the runway. This tendency could be counteracted only after attaining sufficient ground speed for rudder utilization, or V_{mcg} (minimum controlled ground speed with an outboard engine inoperative); otherwise, the takeoff had to be abandoned. V_{mcg} speeds on the Convair often exceeded normal V_1 speeds (V_1 = the minimum speed necessary to continue the takeoff roll with one engine inoperative). In such cases, V_1 was increased to five percent over the V_{mcg} speed. The basic 880 model rudder was not particularly effective. In addition to being manually operated, its size and location on the end of a shorter fuselage than that of the 707 or DC-8 were also factors. As noted earlier, the 880M model incorporated a hydraulically power-assisted rudder which helped somewhat.

Once committed to takeoff, the pilot still had his hands full when an engine failed. He had only 2.5 seconds to apply full rudder or lose directional control. The airplane would turn towards the dead engine and, if too close to the ground, could not be recovered. This procedure was taught under actual conditions. The instructor would normally reduce power on an outboard engine just after V_{mcg} and before or immediately after V_1 was attained.

Four training accidents occurred during this phase of instruction.

May 23, 1960: msn 16 - N8804E, Atlanta, Ga.

Just eight days after the 880 had begun revenue service, Delta Air Lines Training Flight 1903 was lost at Atlanta Hartsfield International Airport; the airplane had accumulated only 127 flying hours.

Immediately after takeoff, the 880 assumed an extremely nose-high attitude and banked steeply to the left, then rolled to the right, stalled, and struck the ground. The four crewmen aboard were killed.

It was determined that the Number Four engine had been throttled back to idle power sometime during takeoff (Cockpit voice recorders were not yet in use). The pilot, apparently over-correcting for the power loss, was at too low an altitude to recover.

During the investigation it was discovered that the captain had probably suffered a heart attack, but pathologists were unable to determine whether it occurred before or as a result of the accident.

Sept. 13, 1965: msn 26 - N820TW, Mid-Continent Airport, Kansas City, Mo.

The TWA training flight was taking off to the north, practicing a critical engine-out scenario. When normal corrective action did not prevent the airplane from drifting to one side of the runway, power was cut to the opposite engine, allowing partial control to be regained, but the crew was unable to stop on the runway. N820TW settled to the ground in a corn field beyond the airport and was destroyed by fire. The three crew members escaped uninjured, but a brand new airport fire truck which responded to the crash become mired in mud and was also lost when the flames spread.

An investigation revealed that the wing spoilers had failed to completely retract on one

Jon Proctor Collection

side following a routine pre-takeoff check. This, together with the simulated engine loss, made the aircraft uncontrollable. A modification was subsequently completed on all 880s to prevent a recurrence of the retraction failure.

Aug. 26, 1966: msn 45 (M) - JA8030, Tokyo-Haneda Airport, Japan

As with the Delta and TWA accidents, this JAL training flight was on its takeoff roll and practicing engine-out procedures. Directional control was lost as the airplane lifted off, and it crashed back onto the runway, catching fire immediately. The five pilots were killed.

June 24, 1969: msn 49 (M) - JA8023, Moses Lake, Wash.

The JAL pilot check flight was simulating an engine-out takeoff when directional control was lost. Three were killed, and the aircraft was destroyed. (As of this writing, JAL still maintains a pilot training facility at Moses Lake.)

In 1969, the National Transportation Safety Board (NTSB) strongly recommended that simulated engine-out training, when conducted under actual flight conditions, be accomplished at a safe altitude to allow recovery without endangering the aircraft and crew members. Thanks to today's modern flight simulators these scenarios are rarely practiced in commercial airliners.

Other Hull Losses

Feb. 27, 1965: msn 59 (M) - JA8023, Iki Island, Kyusyu, Japan

While practicing approach and go-around procedures during a training flight, the Japan Air Lines aircraft struck a sea wall and crashed onto an unfinished runway. The crew safely evacuated before the 880 was consumed by fire. One of the pilots was later involved in the Moses Lake crash.

Nov. 5, 1967: msn 37 (M) - VR-HFX, Hong Kong-Kai Tak Airport

Operating a scheduled service, the 880 accelerated normally to 122 knots when it began to vibrate severely and swerve to the right. Unsure of the cause, the captain elected to abort takeoff, but was unable to stop before sliding off the runway, over a sea wall and into the harbor. Of the 116 passengers and 11 crew members aboard, one passenger was killed on impact, and all others escaped with 33 receiving minor injuries. The accident was blamed on a shredded right-hand nose gear tire which rendered the aircraft uncontrollable.

Nov. 21, 1967: msn 27 - N821TW, Covington, Ky.

Operating TWA Flight 128 from Los Angeles to Cincinnati, the crew attempted to land on a runway which did not have an operational instrument landing system, approach lights or middle marker. N821TW impacted approximately two miles from the runway threshold and 15 feet below airport elevation; 70 of the 82 on board died. Among other causes, the National Transportation Safety Board (NTSB) cited the first officer's failure to call out any altitude or airspeed reports and a lack of adherence to the minimum approach altitude.

TWA and the Airline Pilots Association (ALPA) put forth the possibility of a pitot-static port system failure, but the Board disagreed. Nonetheless, TWA obtained the necessary supplemental type certificate and added a static port heater system to its remaining 880s.

June 15, 1972: msn 53 (M) - VR-HFZ, Over Pleiku, South Vietnam

Cathay Pacific Flight 700Z was en route from Bangkok to Hong Kong at 29,000 feet in good weather when radio contact was lost just over an hour after its takeoff from Don Muang Airport. Widely scattered wreckage indicated an in-flight breakup. Seventy-one passengers and a crew of 10 were lost, including the same flight engineer who endured the aborted takeoff accident at Hong Kong.

Although it was initially reported that a mid-air collision had occurred, an investigation revealed that the 880 had been intentionally destroyed by an explosive device placed close to the aircraft center of gravity. A Bangkok police officer was accused of planting the bomb in order to collect on insurance policies he had bought for his common-law wife and daughter who were aboard the flight. He was never convicted.

Dec. 20, 1972: msn 29 - N8807E, Chicago, Ill.

Operating as Delta Flight 954, the 880 had just completed a flight from Tampa, Florida and was taxiing to the terminal with 93 persons aboard. While crossing an active runway, it was struck by a North Central Airlines DC-9-31 which attempted a premature liftoff to avoid a broadside collision. The DC-9 tail skid cut through the top of the Convair's fuselage and its wing snapped off the 880 tail, then crashed back onto the runway.

Nine aboard the North Central flight died, and 15 were injured; the DC-9 was destroyed by fire. Only one Delta passenger was slightly hurt during the 880 evacuation. Although repairable, N8807E was considered damaged beyond economical repair. After being stripped of usable parts, it spent well over a year behind Delta's hangar before succumbing to the welder's torch.

Aug. 21, 1976: msn 47 (M) - N48060, Seletar Airport, Singapore

The Airtrust Singapore aircraft was attempting to take off from the 5,300-foot Seletar Airport runway. Unbeknown to the cockpit crew, a heavy spare parts kit had been moved forward from the rear cargo compartment, placing the aircraft outside its center of gravity limits. Unable to rotate at takeoff speed, the captain aborted, and the 880M ran off the end of the runway. It sustained relatively minor structural damage but, considered uneconomical to repair, was declared a write-off.

Dec. 16, 1976: msn 57 (M) - N5865, Miami, Fla.

En route to the Dominican Republic with 37 milk cows, the Air Trine flight was unable to lift off from Miami International Airport and came to rest in a canal beyond the end of the runway. Apparently the cattle were not adequately penned and moved aft during the takeoff run, causing a tail-heavy condition, then stampeded forward. Two of the three crewmen were injured, including the flight engineer, who was pinned in the wreckage for six hours. The cattle were all either killed or had to be destroyed, and the 880, substantially damaged, was later scrapped.

ATP/Airliners America

Aug. 20, 1977: msn 65 - N8817E, San Jose, Costa Rica

The Monarch Aviation aircraft, on lease to Latin Carga, crashed into a mountain shortly after take-off from San Jose Airport, reportedly because of improper cargo distribution. It was en route to Venezuela with a load of beef. All three crew members were killed.

May 25, 1978: msn 63 - N8815E, Miami, Fla.

N8815E was substantially damaged during a takeoff accident at Miami International Airport while on lease to Groth Air. It came to rest beyond the runway with a collapsed nose gear. There were no injuries to the cockpit crew on this cargo flight. Considered beyond economical repair, the airplane was finally scrapped after sitting at the airport for more than three years.

March 29, 1980: msn 41 - HP-821, Panama City, Panama

While attempting a landing in a rain shower, the Inair cargo aircraft skidded off the runway and into a ditch, incurring substantial damage. It was later scrapped.

Nov. 3, 1980: msn 64 - YV-145C, Caracas, Venezuela

The Latin Carga freighter, operating empty, was lost in a takeoff accident at Simon Bolivar Airport; all four crew members died in the crash.

The 990

Convair's 990 flew safely for its owners, but was involved in more than its share of accidents. However, none of the 11 aircraft losses were directly linked to the airplane's integrity.

Hull Losses

May 30, 1963: msn 28 - N5616 - Newark International Airport, N.J.

Diverted to Newark because of fog at Idlewild Airport, the American Airlines flight from Chicago landed at Newark at 11:50 p.m. Its passengers and their baggage were transported by bus to Idlewild while the 990 was relocated to a ramp away from the terminal building. Around 6 o'clock the following morning, the rear section of the airplane burst into flames. The fire quickly spread forward and consumed most of the cabin interior and mail still

loaded in the cargo compartments. An investigation determined that the blaze was probably caused by a smoldering cigarette left in an aft lavatory trash container. Although major components were salvaged, the plane was written off and scrapped.

May 28, 1968: msn 03 - PK-GJA - Nalla Sopora, India

All 29 passengers and crew were killed, along with one person on the ground, when the Garuda flight went down 20 miles from Bombay's Santa Cruz Airport, shortly after takeoff. Although little information was found on the accident, the 990 was reportedly approaching the speed of sound when it hit the ground in a nearly vertical attitude. One source speculated that sabotage caused the crash.

Dec. 28, 1968: msn 10 & 31 - OD-AEX/OD-AEW - Beirut, Lebanon

During a spectacular raid at Beirut International Airport, an Israeli commando unit destroyed 13 Lebanese airliners in retaliation for an attack two days earlier by the Arab Palestine Liberation Front, against an El Al flight at Athens, Greece. The plane had been machine-gunned, killing one passenger and injuring a stewardess.

Arriving at Beirut during the night in four helicopters, the Israeli group placed plastic-explosive charges in the landing gear compartments of each aircraft, including both of Lebanese International Airways' 990s, and blew them up. There were no casualties. Among the other aircraft destroyed was a brand new MEA 707, delivered from the factory only 10 days earlier.

Jan. 5, 1970: msn 32 - EC-BNM - Arlanda, Sweden

Operating a charter flight earlier in the day, the Spantax 990 had departed from Stockholm for Las Palmas, but returned with engine problems. A decision was made to operate a three-engine ferry flight to Zürich for repairs, carrying only the crew of 10. Shortly after takeoff in heavy fog, the airplane crashed into a forest. Five aboard survived, including a stewardess who crawled back into the wreckage after being thrown clear on impact, and radioed for help on a portable transmitter.

Feb. 21, 1970: msn 15 - HB-ICD - near Zürich, Switzerland

Only moments after departing Kloten Airport for Tel Aviv, the pilot of Swissair flight SR330 radioed that he suspected an explosion had occurred in the Coronado's aft baggage compartment. Because of low ceilings, he was forced to circle for an instrument approach and lost control before a landing could be completed. The plane crashed into woods near the village of Wüerenlingen 25 miles from Zürich, killing the 38 passengers and nine crew members. An investigation revealed that the explosion was caused by a bomb, placed in a passenger suitcase.

Aug. 8, 1970: msn 13 - N5603 - Acapulco, Mexico

Because Mexican inclusive tour rules required groups to arrive by air at one city and depart from another, the Modern Air Transport 990 was landing at Acapulco without passengers when it slid off the runway late at night in a rainstorm, and broke up. Seven injured crew members were taken to the hospital. As they began to regain consciousness the following morning, it was discovered that an eighth member of the crew — a stewardess — was unaccounted for. Returning to the wreck, workers discovered the overlooked woman, badly injured and pinned in the tail section. She had also endured a short-circuit fire during the night.

Dec. 3, 1972: msn 25 - EC-BZR - Santa Cruz de Tenerife, Canary Islands

Departing Los Rodeos Airport for Münich, the Spantax charter flight lifted off briefly, then crashed from an altitude of 300 feet, hitting the ground 1,000 feet beyond the runway; all 148 passengers and seven crew members were killed. A loss of control by the co-pilot, believed to have occurred as a result of zero visibility conditions, was given as the accident's cause. The cockpit data recorder showed that the aircraft rotated for takeoff about 20 knots below the normal takeoff speed. Luckily, an apprehensive couple already aboard the plane at departure time, had gotten off at the last minute, and were the only survivors of the charter group.

April 12, 1973: msn 01 - N711NA - Sunnyvale, Calif.

Returning from a research mission, NASA's *Galileo* research aircraft collided with a U.S. Navy Lockheed P-3 Orion antisubmarine aircraft at an altitude of approximately 300 feet. Both planes, on approach to Moffett Field, crashed onto the Sunnyvale Municipal Golf Course killing 17, including 11 on the 990.

Sept. 10, 1973: msn 04 - N7876 - Agana, Guam

The ex-Garuda aircraft was being ferried to the United States for sale to NASA when it suffered substantial damage while landing for fuel at the Agana Naval Air Station on the island of Guam. A heavy rainstorm was passing over the approach course with runway crosswinds gusting to 20 knots. A hard landing collapsed the left main landing gear and the aircraft came to rest against a fuel truck on the ramp; there was no fire. N7876, considered damaged beyond economical repair, was scrapped.

July 17, 1985: msn 37 - N712NA - March Air Force Base, Calif.

NASA's *Galileo II* was taking off when one of the landing gear tires failed. Although the flight was successfully aborted, debris from the blowout penetrated a fuel tank, igniting a fire. The four crew members and 15 scientists, well-drilled in evacuation procedures, quickly escaped without injury, however the airplane was destroyed.

Honorable mention should be given to Spantax 990 EC-BJC (msn 22). It collided with an Iberia DC-9-32 (EC-BII) over Nantes, France on March 5, 1973. The DC-9 crashed, killing all 68 aboard. However, the Convair managed to land safely at a nearby military airport with 18 feet of wing missing and the hydraulic system disabled. It was returned to service following repairs.

PART IV

AIRCRAFT PRODUCTION LIST

The individual aircraft histories which follow are formatted with the goal of simplicity. In many cases it was not possible to determine through government or private records whether a registered name was that of an airline, owner, or simply a "paper" company. Corporate name changes have been deleted, with only the original identity supplied. For example, American Jet Industries was merged into Gulfstream American a year after acquiring 16 of TWA's 880s, and the successor company name has not been included in this list unless an initial transaction took place after the name change. The airport code MCI has been substituted for Kansas City Mid-Continent Airport. Hughes Tool Company is referred to as "Toolco." In cases where an ownership change is uncertain, the preface "To" is made, rather than S (sold) or L (leased).

Individual aircraft are listed by the manufacturer's serial number (msn), or "constructor's number," which coincides with the "line number," or order in which completed aircraft came off the assembly line. Also included is Convair's version number (VN) consisting of three parts. First is the model (22 or 30), common to all, followed by the airline version , i.e. 1, 2, etc., then the total number of that version which the aircraft represents (see below). For example, VN 22-1-6 indicates Model 22 (880), airline version 1 (TWA), and the sixth in that version produced.

Delivery dates generally indicate when the title changed from Convair to the customer, and do not always reflect delivery flight dates. Leases from the manufacturer were normally from Convair's parent corporation, General Dynamics (GD).

Other standard abbreviations, incorporated to conserve space, are:

A -	accepted	**R -**	registered
CS -	color scheme	**RR -**	re-registered
D -	delivered	**RO -**	roll-out
DBR -	damaged beyond economical repair	**RFS -**	retired from service
		RTS -	returned to service
FF-	first flight date	**S -**	sold
IS -	in service date	**TT -**	total flying time
L -	leased	**WFU -**	withdrawn from use

Convair 880 Original Version Numbers:

22-1 -	Hughes Tool Co.	22-4 -	Civil Air Transport
22-2 -	Delta	22-21 -	VIASA, Alaska, FAA
22-3 -	Capital, Cathay Pacific	22-22 -	Japan Air Lines

Convair 990 Original Version Numbers:

30-5	American
30-6	Swissair
30-8	VARIG

Convair 880

MSN: 1   VN: 22-1-1

N801TW: RO 12/15/59 in CV colors. House airplane. FF 1/27/59. Assigned to flight test/certification program.
N8489H: Converted to CV-880M for re-certification program in 1961. S to TWA; D 10/29/64; TT 750.9 hrs.
N871TW: Reconfigured to standard 880 version at MCI and RR; IS 5/28/65. RFS 11/1/73 and stored at MCI; TT 23,800 hrs.; 14,517 landings.
N880AJ: S to American Jet Industries 4/18/78; RR 8/8/78. Ferried to Harlingen, TX 9/21/78. Transferred to Mojave, CA for storage 1980; TT as of 10/89: 23,801 hrs.; 14,520 landings. S to Charlotte Aerospace 6/85. Cockpit section removed and trucked to Atlanta for refurbishment by Delta Air Lines employees. Placed on permanent display at Atlanta Heritage Row Expo, Atlanta underground; Summer 1990. Portion of center fuselage shipped to Minneapolis, MN for use in film on United DC-10 Sioux City crash; balance of aircraft scrapped at Mojave. *(Clay Jansson)*

(**Note:** *The second fuselage off the assembly line, with wing stubs only, was used for fatigue testing and not assigned a serial number. After completion of the certification program, it was transported by rail to the FAA Technical Center at Atlantic City, N.J. for further testing, then broken up.*)

MSN: 2   VN: 22-1-2

N802TW: Proof test aircraft; used for stress testing in certification program. Stored at San Diego, pending Toolco financing. S to TWA; D 3/18/61; TT 11.5 hrs. IS 4/14/61. RFS 4/10/74 and stored at MCI. TT 34,440 hrs., 19,769 landings. S to Kansas City Recycling and scrapped fall 1979 at MCI. *(Clay Jansson)*

MSN: 3   VN: 22-1-3

N803TW: FF 3/31/59, in GD colors. Assigned to flight test/certification program. Stored at San Diego, pending Toolco financing. S to TWA; D 10/13/61; TT 542.5 hrs.; IS 10/20/61. RFS 1/7/74 and stored at MCI; TT 33,410 hrs., 19,857 landings.
N801AJ: S to American Jet Industries 4/18/78; RR 6/21/78. Ferried to Harlingen, TX 7/25/78. Transferred to Mojave, CA for storage 1980. S to Charlotte Aerospace 6/85. S to Federal Aviation Administration and ferried to Atlantic City, NJ 9/9/91 for burn testing with FAA Fire Safety Branch. Extant. *(Clay Jansson)*

MSN: 4 VN: 22-2-1

N8801E: FF 8/10/59, in GD colors. D to Delta 12/12/60. IS same day. Traded in to Boeing. RFS 12/8/73 and handed over at Wichita, KS same day; TT 39,989.9 hrs.

AN-BLW: To LANICA via Orion Jet Sales 4/74. RFS and stored at Miami, FL 3/23/75. S to Summa Corp. 11/26/78.

N817AJ: S to American Jet Industries; RR 2/5/79. Freighter conversion commenced 4/79 (probably at Miami). To Ligonair; date unknown. Operated by Central American Airways on behalf of Profit Express/Profit Airlines 7/24/81. Repainted in Profit Express colors 8/3/81. RFS 12/84 and stored (location/condition unknown). *(Clay Jansson)*

MSN: 5 VN: 22-1-4

N804TW: For 9/59 del. to TWA; stored at San Diego pending Toolco financing.

N8478H: L to Northeast by GD 1/21/61. Returned 9/10/63.

N804TW: S to TWA; D 9/11/63 at Boston; TT 7,190 hrs.; IS 9/24/63. RFS 10/24/73 and stored at MCI; TT 33,624 hrs.; 16,282 landings. S to Kansas City Recycling and scrapped fall 1979 at MCI.

(Clay Jansson)

MSN: 6 VN: 22-1-5

N805TW: For 10/60 del. to TWA; stored at San Diego pending Toolco financing. S to TWA; D 8/10/61; IS 8/18/61. RFS 1/7/74 and stored at MCI; TT 33,540 hrs., 20,085 landings.

N802AJ: S to American Jet Industries 4/18/78; RR 6/21/78. Ferried to Harlingen, TX 7/24/78. Transferred to Van Nuys, CA; main deck cargo door installed. Transferred to Mojave, CA for storage 1980. S to Charlotte Aerospace 6/85. S to Torco Oil Co. 12/93. Extant (in basic TWA CS). *(General Dynamics)*

MSN: 7   VN: 22-2-2

N8802E: D 1/31/60 to Delta (ceremonial acceptance 2/10/60); first customer delivery aircraft; named *Delta Queen*. IS 5/15/60. Traded in to Boeing; RFS 11/16/73 and handed over at Wichita, KS same day; TT 41,087.3 hrs. S to Transexecutive Aviation; D 10/23/74. S to Louis A. Galvao, Fall River, MA 10/26/74.

N55NW: RR 12/2/74. S back to Transexecutive Aviation 3/25/75. L to Bahamas World 6/76. L to ECB Leasing 1978. Converted to cargo configuration; no main deck cargo door. S to Worldwide Air Leases, Inc. 12/6/78. L to Groth Air Services 1/15/79.

N880SR: RR 12/13/79 and repainted in blue CS. Impounded at Mexico City. Destroyed by fire May 1983 at Mexico City under suspicious circumstances.   *(Jon Proctor Collection)*

MSN: 8   VN: 22-1-6

N806TW: For TWA; stored at San Diego pending Toolco financing.

N8479H: L to Northeast by GD; D 1/30/61. Returned to GD 9/63.

N806TW: S to TWA; D 9/12/63 at Boston; TT 7,160 hrs.; IS 9/30/63. RFS 1/7/74 and stored at MCI; TT 35,011 hrs.; 17,604 landings.

N803AJ: S to American Jet Industries 4/18/78; RR 8/8/78. Ferried to Harlingen, TX 9/19/78. Transferred to Mojave, CA for storage 1980. S to Charlotte Aerospace 6/85. S to Torco Oil Co. 12/93. Extant (in basic TWA CS).   *(Clay Jansson)*

MSN: 9   VN: 22-1-7

N807TW: For 10/61 del. to TWA; stored at San Diego pending Toolco financing.

N8492H: D to Toolco 5/3/62 and ferried to Ontario, CA for storage. L to Northeast 9/10/63. Returned 1/19/68 and stored at Ontario.

AN-BIB: L to (and later purchased by) LANICA 5/23/72. Ferried to Kansas City 8/22/72 after refurbishing. Crew training conducted in the U.S. RFS 2/75 and stored at Miami, FL.

N90452: To Summa Corp. (successor to Toolco) 11/78.

N818AJ: S to American Jet Industries 12/28/78. Scrapped 12/17/81 at Miami (still wearing AN-BIB registration).   *(General Dynamics)*

MSN: 10   VN: 22-1-8

N808TW: S directly to TWA; D 5/18/60; TT 21 hrs. Flown without airline colors during crew training and route proving. Painted and placed into revenue service 1/14/61. RFS 1/14/74 and stored at MCI; TT 36,505 hrs., 19,594 landings.

N804AJ: S to American Jet Industries 4/18/78; RR 6/7/78. Ferried to Harlingen, TX 6/23/78. Transferred to Mojave, CA for storage 1980. S to Charlotte Aerospace 6/85. S to Federal Aviation Administration and ferried to Atlantic City, NJ 3/8/89. Intentionally burned to destruction 10/30/89 to replicate a 1985 British Airtours Boeing 737 accident.   *(Clay Jansson)*

MSN: 11   VN: 22-2-3

N8803E: D to Delta 5/4/60; IS 5/15/60. Traded in to Boeing; RFS 11/17/73 and handed over at Wichita, KS same day; TT 40,482.8 hrs.

N880NW: S to Transexecutive Aviation; D 11/8/74 and stored at Miami. S to Louis A. Galvao 1974. S to American Jet Industries. Scrapped 4/26/83 at Miami.   *(Clay Jansson)*

MSN: 12   VN: 22-1-9

N809TW: For TWA; stored at San Diego pending Toolco financing.

N8480H: L to Northeast by GD; D 12/14/60. Returned 7/63.

N809TW: S to TWA; D 7/29/63 at Ontario, CA; TT 6,890 hrs.; IS 8/18/63. RFS 6/13/74 and stored at MCI; TT 35,356 hrs.; 18,128 landings.

N806AJ: S to American Jet Industries 4/18/78; ferried to Harlingen, TX 7/21/78. Transferred to Mojave, CA for storage 1980. S to Charlotte Aerospace 6/85. Stored at Laurinburg, NC. Registration reported canceled 12/89. Broken up; date unknown.   *(Clay Jansson)*

MSN: 13   VN 22-1-10

N810TW: For 7/60 del. to TWA; stored at San Diego pending Toolco financing. S to TWA; D 2/15/61; TT 19.1 hrs.; IS 3/16/61. RFS 8/10/73 and stored at MCI; TT 33,459 hrs., 18,534 landings.

N807AJ: S to American Jet Industries 4/18/78; RR 8/8/78. Ferried to Harlingen, TX 9/20/78. Transferred to Mojave, CA for storage 1980. S to Charlotte Aerospace 6/85. S to FAA and ferried to Atlantic City, NJ 9/18/91 for burn testing at FAA Fire Safety Branch. Extant.   *(Jon Proctor Collection)*

MSN: 14   VN: 22-1-11

N811TW: For 7/60 del. to TWA; stored at San Diego pending Toolco financing. S to TWA; D 2/2/61; TT 13.3 hrs.; IS 2/10/61. RFS 11/2/72 and stored at MCI; TT 32,123 hrs., 17,947 landings. S to Kansas City Recycling 5/24/77 and scrapped at MCI.

(Jay Sherlock)

MSN: 15   VN: 22-1-12

N812TW: For 8/60 del. to TWA; stored at San Diego pending Toolco financing. S to TWA; D 6/9/61; TT 14.1 hrs.; IS 6/15/61. RFS 1/6/74 and stored at MCI; TT 34,071 hrs., 19,621 landings.

N808AJ: S to American Jet Industries 4/18/78; RR 6/21/78. Ferried to Harlingen, TX 7/22/78. Transferred to Mojave, CA for storage 1980. S to Charlotte Aerospace 6/85. S to Torco Oil Co. 12/93. Extant (in basic TWA CS).   *(Jon Proctor)*

MSN: 16   VN: 22-2-4

N8804E: D to Delta 5/6/60; IS 5/15/60. Destroyed in training accident at Atlanta 5/23/60; TT 127 hrs.   *(Jon Proctor Collection)*

MSN: 17   VN: 22-2-5

N8805E: D to Delta 6/2/60; IS 6/4/60. Traded in to Boeing; RFS 12/8/73 and handed over at Wichita, KS same day; TT 40,958.8 hrs.

N800NW: S to Transexecutive Aviation; D 11/8/74 and stored at Marana, AZ.

N8805E: S to Onyx Aviation, Inc. 4/7/78; RR 5/2/78. S to Patterson Aircraft Corp. 12/16/81. L to Seagreen Air Transport 1/82. Main deck cargo door installed at Miami by General Air Services 5/82.

HH-SMA: S to Haiti Air Freight; RR 5/85. WFU (date unknown) and stored at Port-au-Prince, Haiti. Extant.

(Clay Jansson)

MSN: 18   VN 22-1-13

N813TW: For 10/60 del. to TWA; stored at San Diego pending Tool Co. financing.

N8493H: D to Toolco 5/3/62 and Stored at Ontario, CA. L to Northeast 8/8/63. Returned 1/24/68 and stored at Marana, AZ. S to California Airmotive 7/24/74 and stored at Van Nuys, CA. To American Jet Industries 1975. Main deck cargo door installed 9/78 at Van Nuys (first to receive AJI conversion). S to Potter Aircraft Co. 7/81, operating as Flying Fish Co.; named *El Pajaro*. WFU and parked at St. Johns, Newfoundland, then ferried to Mojave, CA (via Detroit) for storage. S to Charlotte Aerospace 1985. S to Torco Oil Co. 12/93. Extant (bare metal).

(J. Stewart)

MSN: 19   VN: 22-1-14

N814TW: For 8/60 del. to TWA; stored at San Diego pending Tool Co. financing. S to TWA; D 9/2/61; TT 13.2 hr.; IS 9/8/61. RFS 1/6/74 and stored at MCI; TT 33,568 hrs., 19,523 landings. **N809AJ:** S to American Jet Industries 4/18/78; RR 6/21/78. Ferried to Harlingen, TX 7/23/78. Transferred to Van Nuys; main deck cargo door installed. Transferred to Mojave, CA for storage 1980. S to Charlotte Aerospace 6/85. S to Torco Oil Co. 12/93. Extant (in basic TWA CS). *(Jon Proctor)*

MSN: 20   VN: 22-1-15

N815TW: For TWA; stored at San Diego pending Tool Co. financing.
N8481H: L to Northeast by GD; D 12/8/60. Returned 8/63.
N815TW: S to TWA; D 8/26/63 at Boston; TT 7,415 hrs.; IS 9/8/63. RFS 1/9/74 and stored at MCI; TT 35,629 hrs., 18,044 landings.
N810AJ: S to American Jet Industries 4/18/78; RR 6/7/78. Ferried to Harlingen, TX 6/24/78. Transferred to Mojave, CA for storage 1980. S to Charlotte Aerospace 6/85. S to Torco Oil Co. 12/93. Extant (in basic TWA CS). *(John Wegg Collection)*

MSN: 21   VN: 22-2-6

N8806E: D to Delta 7/4/60; IS 7/7/60. Traded in to Boeing; RFS 12/18/73 and handed over at Wichita, KS same day; TT 44,081 hrs. S to Orion Jet Sales, Houston, TX; D 6/15/74. S to Onyx Aviation, Inc. 1/20/76; converted to cargo configuration (no main deck cargo door). L to Concordia Corp. of Greece 5/77. Abandoned at Lisbon 5/4/80. Sold at auction and converted to a restaurant near Lisbon Airport. Extant. *(Delta)*

MSN: 22   VN: 22-1-16

N816TW: For TWA; stored at San Diego pending Toolco financing.
N8482H: L to Northeast by GD; D 12/5/60. Returned 9/63.
N816TW: S to TWA; D 9/13/63 at Boston; TT 7,430 hrs.; IS 10/4/63. RFS 6/11/74 and stored at MCI; TT 35,606 hrs., 17,554 landings.
N811AJ: S to American Jet Industries 4/18/78; RR 6/23/78. Ferried to Harlingen, TX 7/20/78. Transferred to Mojave, CA for storage 1980. S to Charlotte Aerospace 6/85. S to Torco Oil Co. 12/93. Extant (in basic TWA CS).   *(G. Pennick)*

MSN: 23   VN: 22-1-17

N817TW: For TWA; stored at San Diego pending Toolco financing.
N8483H: L to Northeast by GD; D 11/30/60. Returned 7/63.
N817TW: S to TWA; D 7/29/63 at Ontario, CA; TT 6,837 hrs.; IS 8/24/63. RFS 5/31/74 and stored at MCI; TT 35,201 hrs., 17,704 landings.
N812AJ: S to American Jet Industries 4/18/78; RR 6/12/78. Ferried to Harlingen, TX 6/25/78. Transferred to Mojave, CA for storage 1980. S to Charlotte Aerospace 6/85. S to Warner Brothers Inc. 9/90. Painted in blue/gold CS for movie *The Rookie*. S to Aviation Warehouse. Extant (in blue/gold CS; no titles).   *(Jon Proctor Collection)*

MSN: 24
VN: 22-1-18

N818TW: For 6/60 del. to TWA; stored at San Diego pending Toolco financing. S to TWA; D 1/5/61; TT 41.5 hrs.; IS 1/12/61. RFS 6/14/74 and stored at MCI; TT 34,912 hrs., 19,245 landings.
N813AJ: S to American Jet Industries 4/18/78; RR 6/6/78. Ferried to Van Nuys, CA 6/7/78; main deck cargo door installed. Transferred to Mojave, CA for storage. S to Charlotte Aerospace 6/85. S to Torco Oil Co. 12/93. Extant (bare metal).   *(Peter W. Black)*

MSN: 25 VN: 22-1-19

N819TW: For 6/60 del. to TWA; stored at San Diego pending Toolco financing. S to TWA; D 1/12/61; TT 30.4 hrs.; IS 1/22/61. RFS 1/8/74 and stored at MCI; TT 34,837 hrs., 19,639 landings. S to Kansas City Recycling and scrapped Fall 1979 at MCI.

(Tom Hildreth)

MSN: 26 VN: 22-1-20

N820TW: For 8/60 del. to TWA; stored at San Diego pending Toolco financing. S to TWA; D 3/20/61; TT 21.1 hrs.; IS 4/1/61. Destroyed in training accident 9/13/65 at MCI; TT 12,324 hrs.

(Clay Jansson)

MSN: 27 VN: 22-1-21

N821TW: For 6/60 del. to TWA; stored at San Diego pending Toolco financing. S to TWA; D 1/8/61; TT 27.5 hrs.; IS 1/12/61. Destroyed 11/21/67 in landing accident at Covington, KY; TT 18,850 hrs.

(Jon Proctor)

MSN: 28 VN: 22-1-22

N822TW: For 7/60 del. to TWA; stored at San Diego pending Toolco financing. S to TWA; D 1/6/61; TT 16.7 hrs.; IS 1/12/61. RFS 6/15/74 and stored at MCI; TT 35,632 hrs., 19,754 landings. S to Kansas City Recycling and scrapped Fall 1979 at MCI.

(Clay Jansson)

MSN: 29   VN: 22-2-7

N8807E: D 8/5/60 to Delta; IS 8/7/60. DBR 12/20/72 in ground collision with a North Central DC-9-31 at Chicago-O'Hare; TT 37,640.1 hrs. Sold to insurance company summer 1973 and scrapped at O'Hare.

(Clay Jansson)

MSN: 30   VN: 22-1-23

N823TW: For 7/60 del. to TWA; stored at San Diego pending Toolco financing. S to TWA; D 3/15/61; TT 29.3 hrs.; IS 3/30/61. RFS 1/8/74 and stored at MCI; TT 34,917 hrs., 20,065 landings. S to Kansas City Recycling and scrapped fall 1979 at MCI.

(Jay Sherlock)

MSN: 31   VN: 22-1-24

N824TW: For 10/60 del. to TWA; stored at San Diego pending Toolco financing. S to TWA; D 1/1/61; TT 18.5 hrs.; IS 1/12/61. Operated TWA's last scheduled 880 service on 6/15/74. WFU same day and stored at MCI; TT 34,197 hrs., 19,417 landings. S to Kansas City Recycling and scrapped fall 1979 at MCI.

(Clay Jansson)

MSN: 32   VN: 22-1-25

N825TW: For 10/60 del. to TWA; stored at San Diego pending Toolco financing. S to TWA; D 1/21/61; TT 12.5 hrs.; IS 1/25/61. RFS 1/6/74 and stored at MCI; TT 34,652 hrs., 19,708 landings. **N814AJ:** S to American Jet Industries 4/18/78; RR 6/12/78. Ferried to Harlingen, TX 6/26/78. Transferred to Mojave, CA for storage 1980; passenger windows and interior removed but cargo

door not installed. S to Charlotte Aerospace 6/85. Fictitious Pan West titles, logo and N375 registration applied for 1986 *Amazing Stories* television series. S to Torco Oil Co. 12/93. Extant (still wearing Pan West/TWA livery).

(Clay Jansson)

MSN: 33 VN: 22-1-26

N826TW: For 8/60 del. to TWA; stored at San Diego pending Toolco financing. S to TWA; D 5/6/61; TT 27.3 hrs.; IS 5/20/61. RFS 1/16/74 and stored at MCI; TT 34,161 hrs., 19,408 landings. S to Kansas City Recycling and scrapped fall 1979 at MCI.

(Clay Jansson)

MSN: 34 VN: 22-1-27

N827TW: For 7/61 del. to TWA; stored at San Diego pending Toolco financing.
N8494H: D to Toolco 5/9/62 and stored at Ontario, CA. L to Northeast; D 10/25/62. Returned 2/24/68 and stored at Marana, AZ. Moved to Burbank, CA early 1974. To California Airmotive 7/74. To American Jet Industries 1975. Main deck cargo door installed at Van Nuys. Transferred to Mojave, CA for storage; TT 14,966 hrs. S to Charlotte Aerospace 6/85. S to Torco Oil Co. 12/93. Extant (bare metal).

(Jon Proctor Collection)

MSN: 35 VN: 22-1-28

N828TW: For 8/60 del. to TWA; stored at San Diego pending Toolco financing. S to TWA; D 4/26/61; TT 22.7 hrs.; IS 4/30/61. RFS 4/29/74 and stored at MCI; TT 34,727 hrs., 19,755 landings.
N815AJ: S to American Jet Industries 4/18/78; RR 6/19/78. Ferried to Harlingen, TX 6/27/78. Transferred to Mojave, CA for storage 1980. S to Charlotte Aerospace 6/85. S to Torco Oil Co. 12/93. Extant (in basic TWA CS).

(Clay Jansson)

MSN: 36   VN: 22-2-8

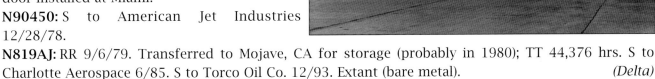

N8808E: D to Delta 10/1/60; IS 10/2/60. Traded in to Boeing; RFS 1/1/74 and handed over at Wichita, KS 1/11/74; TT 39,945.6 hrs.
AN-BLX: S to LANICA via Orion Jet Sales 3/27/74. RFS 6/77 and stored at Miami, FL. S to Summa Corp. 11/26/78. Main deck cargo door installed at Miami.
N90450: S to American Jet Industries 12/28/78.
N819AJ: RR 9/6/79. Transferred to Mojave, CA for storage (probably in 1980); TT 44,376 hrs. S to Charlotte Aerospace 6/85. S to Torco Oil Co. 12/93. Extant (bare metal).   *(Delta)*

MSN: 37 (M)   VN: 22-3-1

(Originally a Capital Airlines delivery position)
N8487H: First production CV-880M. Under U.S. registration for flight testing; used for 880M certification program. All white on RO; no CS.
YV-C-VIC: L to VIASA; D 4/19/63. In joint VIASA/KLM colors (VIASA port, KLM starboard). Operated by VIASA and sub-leased to KLM on single flight basis.
VR-HFX: S to Cathay Pacific 11/65. Destroyed 11/5/67 in takeoff accident at Hong Kong-Kai Tak.
   (Peter W. Black)

MSN: 38   VN: 22-2-9

N8809E: D to Delta 10/22/61; IS 10/26/61. Traded in to Boeing; RFS 1/1/74 and handed over at Wichita, KS 1/10/74; TT 40,270.7 hrs. S to Nigel Winfield 4/17/75.
N880EP: S to Elvis Presley 4/18/75; named *Lisa Marie.* RR to LM Corp. following Presley's death. WFU and stored 1/20/79; for sale. Ferried from Ft. Lauderdale, FL to Memphis, TN 2/6/84 and placed on permanent display at Graceland Museum. Extant.
   (J. Stewart)

MSN: 39   VN: 22-1-29

N829TW: For 8/61 del. to TWA; stored at San Diego pending Toolco financing.
N8495H: D to Toolco 5/11/62 and ferried to Ontario, CA for storage. L to Northeast; D 12/1/62. Sub-leased to TWA; D 5/22/67 at Hartford, CT; TT 13,125 hrs.; returned to NE at Miami 11/4/67. Returned to Toolco 2/2/68 and stored at Marana, AZ.
AN-BIA: L to (and later purchased by) LANICA; D 7/10/72. RFS 2/75 and stored at Miami, FL.
N90455: S to Summa Corp. (successor to Toolco) 11/78.
N820AJ: S to American Jet Industries 12/28/78. S to Eight Twenty AJ Corp. (Ligonair) 8/81. Scrapped 11/21/83 at Miami (still wearing AN-BIA registration). *(Jon Proctor Collection)*

MSN: 40   VN: 22-1-30

N830TW: For 10/60 del. to TWA; stored at San Diego pending Toolco financing. S to TWA; D 5/25/61; IS 6/1/61. RFS 4/15/74 and stored at MCI; TT 34,214 hrs., 20,196 landings.
N816AJ: S to American Jet Industries 4/18/78; RR 6/21/78. Ferried to Harlingen, TX 7/19/78. Transferred to Van Nuys; main deck cargo door installed. Transferred to Mojave, CA for storage 1980. S to Charlotte Aerospace 6/85. S to Torco Oil Co. 12/93. Extant (in basic TWA CS).

(Clay Jansson)

MSN: 41   VN: 22-2-10

N8810E: D 11/21/60 to Delta; IS 11/24/60. Traded in to Boeing; RFS 1/1/74 and handed over at Wichita, KS 1/14/74; TT 40,122.1 hrs. S to Aircraft Investors Retaining Corp. 6/23/75 and stored at Burbank, CA. L to Monarch Aviation 8/26/77; D 10/18/77 at Miami, FL. Main deck cargo door installed at Miami 4/78.
HP-821: Sub-L to Inair Panamá; IS 2/6/79. DBR 3/29/80 in landing accident, Panama City, Panama. *(Jon Proctor Collection)*

MSN: 42　　VN: 22-1-31

N801TW: For 9/60 del. to TWA; stored at San Diego pending Toolco financing. S to TWA; D 7/9/61; IS 7/91/61. RFS 6/14/74 and stored at MCI; TT 34,500 hrs., 20,497 landings. S to Kansas City Recycling and scrapped fall 1979 at MCI. *(Clay Jansson)*

(**Note:** *This was the second 880 assigned the N801TW registration. MSN 1 never wore TWA colors.*)

MSN: 43 (M)　　VN: 22-3-2

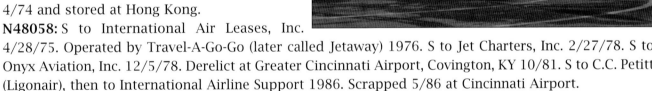

(Originally a Capital Airlines delivery position)
N94284: Under U.S. registration for flight testing.
HB-ICL: L to Swissair by GD; D 8/11/61.
N94284: Returned 5/12/62 and stored at San Diego.
VR-HFT: S to Cathay Pacific; D 10/15/64. RFS 4/74 and stored at Hong Kong.
N48058: S to International Air Leases, Inc.
4/28/75. Operated by Travel-A-Go-Go (later called Jetaway) 1976. S to Jet Charters, Inc. 2/27/78. S to Onyx Aviation, Inc. 12/5/78. Derelict at Greater Cincinnati Airport, Covington, KY 10/81. S to C.C. Petitt (Ligonair), then to International Airline Support 1986. Scrapped 5/86 at Cincinnati Airport.
(Jon Proctor Collection)

MSN: 44 (M)　　VN: 22-4-1

N8486H: Under U.S. registration for flight testing.
B-1008: S to Civil Air Transport; D 6/6/61.
VR-HGA: S to Cathay Pacific; D 10/1/68.
N48059: S to International. Air Leases, Inc. 4/75. S to Orient Pacific Airways, DBA Airtrust Singapore 9/11/75. Wet-leased to Air Malta Nov. 24, 1976-1979; also operated on behalf of Gulf Air. RFS and stored at Seletar Airport, Singapore 1980. Scrapped there in 1984.
(Jon Proctor Collection)

MSN: 45 (M)   VN: 22-3-3

(Originally a Capital Airlines delivery position)
N94285: Under U.S. registration for flight testing
HB-ICM: L to Swissair by GD; D 8/20/61.
N94285: Returned 5/28/62 and stored at San Diego.
JA8030: L to Japan Domestic Airways by GD; D 1/4/65; named *Gina*. L to Japan Air Lines 5/1/66. Destroyed 8/26/66 in training accident at Tokyo International Airport (still in JDA CS).

(Peter Keating)

MSN: 46 (M)   VN 22-3-4

(Originally a Capital Airlines delivery position)
N8491H: Under U.S. registration for flight testing.
JA8026: S to Japan Air Lines; D 7/3/63; named *Yanagi*. RFS 10/70 and stored at Tokyo.
N5858: S to Boeing 3/20/71 and stored at Wichita, KS. S to Aero American Corp.; D 10/18/71. L to Falair, Inc. 11/71. L to Jonian Airways; stored at Miami, FL 1972. Century 2000 titles applied at Miami 1972 but not operated. S to U.S. Universal, Inc. 3/26/73 and stored at Long Beach, CA. Repossessed 7/12/73. S to Holiday Magic Finland OY 8/22/73. To Philodendrone, Inc. 2/15/75. To Monarch Aviation 5/26/79. To Eight Eighty Partnership (Ligonair) 8/10/79; main deck cargo door installed.
N54CP: To Central American Airways; D 2/2/80. Operated on behalf of Profit Express/Profit Airlines from 7/81-5/82; named *La Isla del Encanto* (Enchanted Island). RFS and stored at San Juan, Puerto Rico 1985. Used for fire training prior to being scrapped around 1990.

(Peter Keating)

MSN: 47 (M)   VN: 22-3-5

(Originally a Capital Airlines delivery position)
VR-HFS: S to Cathay Pacific: D 2/20/62. RFS 4/74 and stored at Hong Kong.
N48060: S to International Air Leases 7/75. S to Orient Pacific Airways, DBA Airtrust Singapore 9/75. DBR 8/21/76 during aborted takeoff at Seletar Airport, Singapore.

(Peter Keating)

MSN: 48 (M)   VN: 22-3-6

(Originally a Capital Airlines delivery position)
JA8027: S to Japan Air Lines; D 3/1/63; named *Sumire.* RFS 10/70 and stored at Tokyo.
N5863: S to Boeing 4/12/71 and stored at Wichita, KS. S to Aero American Corp.; D 8/21/71. S to Glenn W. Turner Enterprises 8/71. APU installed. Flown very little after late 1971; stored at Sanford, FL.
TF-AVB: L to Air Viking 7/31/73. Stored at Opa Locka, FL 11/73-Fall 1974. S to Jimmy Williams Aircraft Sales, Inc. 7/8/74.
N5863: S to Rowan Drilling Co. 12/26/74.
N59RD: RR 2/13/75.
N5863: RR 9/20/79. Name changed to RDC Marine, Inc. To General Air Services, Inc.; RR 7/83. Ferried to Mojave, CA and stored. S to FAA 8/20/86 for antimisting fuel tests. Scrapped 10/86 at Mojave.

(Peter Keating)

MSN: 49 (M)   VN: 22-3-7

(Originally a Capital Airlines delivery position)
JA8028: S to Japan Air Lines; D 3/26/63; named *Kikyo.* Destroyed 6/24/69 in training accident at Moses Lake, WA; TT 14,278 hrs.

(Peter Keating)

MSN: 50   VN: 22-2-11

N8811E: D to Delta 9/8/61; IS 9/9/61. Traded in to Boeing; RFS 11/17/73 and handed over at Wichita, KS same day; TT 37,999.1 hrs. S to Aircraft Investors Retaining Corp. 6/23/75 and stored at Burbank, CA. S to Monarch Aviation 8/77. Main deck cargo door installed. L to Inair Panamá 11/77. L to SERCA Costa Rica 11/84. S to Importaciones y Exportaciones 5/86. RFS and stored at Caracas. Extant.

(C. Buckley)

MSN: 51   VN: 22-2-12

N8812E: D to Delta 9/20/61; IS 9/23/61. Traded in to Boeing; RFS 1/1/74 and handed over at Wichita, KS 1/14/74; TT 37,741.6 hrs.
N880WA: S to Westernair of Albuquerque, NM 12/75. S to Worldwide Air leases 12/76. Converted to cargo configuration; no main deck cargo door. S to F&B Livestock 1978. To Fair Air, Inc. 10/83. To Vincent J. Faix 8/84. Scrapped 11/85 at Miami, FL.   *(Delta)*

MSN: 52   VN: 22-2-13

N8813E: D to Delta 10/24/61; IS 10/25/61. Traded in to Boeing; RFS 12/18/73 and handed over at Wichita, KS 1/11/74; TT 37,757.3 hrs. S to Aircraft Investors Retaining Corp. 6/23/75 and stored at Burbank, CA.. S to Monarch Aviation 8/77. Main deck cargo door installed. L to Aerovías Quisqueyana 2/78 not taken up.
HP-876: L to Inair Panamá 1980. Believed to be stored at Panama City; current status/condition unknown.   *(Clay Jansson)*

MSN: 53 (M) VN 22-21-1

N8490H: Under U.S. registration for flight testing.
YV-C-VIA: D 8/1/61 to VIASA.
VR-HFZ: S to Cathay Pacific; D 7/1/67. Destroyed 6/15/72 by sabotage over Pleiku, South Vietnam.

(Peter Keating)

MSN: 54 (M)   VN: 22-21-2

N8477H: D 7/31/61 to Alaska Airlines; IS 8/30/61.

VR-HFY: S to Cathay Pacific; D 11/5/66. RFS 4/74 and stored at Hong Kong.

N48062: S to International Air Leases 4/29/75. S to Orient Pacific Airways, DBA Airtrust Singapore 11/75. Wet leased to Air Malta Feb. 10, 1977-1979. RFS and stored at Seletar Airport, Singapore. Scrapped there in 1984.

(Curtis Hunslander)

MSN: 55 (M)   VN 22-21-3

N112: D 8/13/61 to the U.S. Federal Aviation Administration (FAA).

N42: RR 1974.

N84790: S to Flight Systems, Inc. 1980.

161572: S to U.S. Navy summer 1981. Based at Naval Air Warfare Center, Aircraft Division, Patuxent River, MD. Fitted with refueling equipment for F/A-18 Hornet development and operating tests. Military designation: UC-880. Also served as command and control platform for Harpoon and Tomahawk cruise missile testing. Last flight 9/30/93; deactivated 10/23/93; TT 12,267 hrs. Used for FAA ground structural integrity tests 1995. To be scrapped at Pax River.

(Jon Proctor)

MSN: 56 (M)   VN 22-21-4

N8488H: Flight tested under U.S. registration.

YV-C-VIB: D 9/28/61 to VIASA.

VR-HGC: S to Cathay Pacific; D 11/22/68. RFS 4/74 and stored at Hong Kong.

N48063: S to International Air Leases, Inc. 4/75. S to Four Winds, Inc. 9/2/75. L to Indy Air late 1977. S to Onyx Aviation 10/78 and converted to freighter configuration (no cargo door). L to Sunjet International. 1/81; operated as Four Winds; TT 33,323.6 hrs., 19,666 landings. Returned 1982. RFS and stored at Miami, FL 1984. S to U.S. Navy and ferried to Patuxent River, MD to serve as spares source for UC-880 (see MSN 55). Used for FAA ground structural integrity tests 1995. To be scrapped at Pax River.   *(Jon Proctor Collection)*

MSN 57 (M)   VN: 22-22-1

JA8021: D 7/21/61 to Japan Air Lines; named *Sakura.* RFS 10/70 and stored at Tokyo.
N5865: S to Boeing 4/22/71 and stored at Wichita, KS. S to Aero American Corp; D 1/12/72.
N1RN: RR 10/6/72. L to Freelandia Travel Club 1973.
N5865: S to International Air Leases, Inc. 4/75. Seen operating with Compass titles 1975. Converted to

freighter configuration (no cargo door) at Miami, FL. L to Air Trine 2.76. DBR in accident at Miami Int'l. 12/16/76. Fuselage transferred to Dade Country Aviation Department at Miami Airport for fire practice 8/9/78. Scrapped 10/4/81 by BCR Salvage.

(Jon Proctor Collection)

MSN: 58 (M)   VN: 22-22-2

JA8022: D 9/1/61 to Japan Air Lines; named *Matsu.*
VR-HGF: S to Cathay Pacific; D 7/1/70. RFS 9/15/75.
N88CH: S to International Air Leases, Inc. 9/16/75; arrived Miami, FL 9/20/75 and stored. S to Jet Aviation 2/27/76; R 3/25/76. Converted by Jet Aviation to executive interior at Basle, Switzerland. S to Hirschmann Corp. 1976. Stored at Newburgh, NY 1/78. S to Orchester, Inc. 4/5/78; R 9/27/78. To Triple D Corp. 1/31/79. S to Sentinel Jets Ltd. 3/79. Named *Starship II.* S to C.C. Petitt, Ligonair 10/81. Aircraft seized at MacArthur Airport, Islip, NY by Hudson General

Co., for non-payment of tie-down fees. Bought and refurbished by Chad Koppie. Re-acquired by Ligonair. S to Ciskei government and ferried to Bulembu Airport (via Miami, Barbados, Cape Verde and Abidjan) 7/87 for President of South African State of Ciskei. Not licensed for use; sold to S. African Dept. of Transportation at auction 10/16/91. S to Billy Nel and moved 6/92 to mobile home site at Bonza Bay, East London, South Africa, painted all green with red and gold cheatlines; named *Pinnochio.* Extant.

(Peter Keating)

MSN: 59 (M)   VN: 22-22-3

JA8023: D 9/8/61 to Japan Air Lines; named *Kaede*. Destroyed 2/27/65 in training accident at Iki Island, Kuyshu, Japan.

(JAL)

MSN: 60 (M)   VN: 22-22-4

JA8024: D 6/7/62 to Japan Air Lines; named *Kiku*.
VR-HGG: S to Cathay Pacific; D 6/26/70.
N880JT: S to International Air Leases, Inc.; R 3/16/76. Bahamas World titles applied 7/76; lease not completed. L to LANICA 8/21/76; in basic Cathay CS with LANICA titles. Returned 11/76. L to Bahamas World 11/76. Impounded at London-Gatwick 12/76. Returned

3/20/77. L to Florida Travel Club 1977. Returned 11/9/78. L to Indy Air 2/24/79. Returned 9/28/79 and stored at Miami, FL; TT 31,239 hrs. Scrapped 4/85 at Miami.   *(JAL)*

MSN: 61 (M) VN: 22-22-5

JA8025: D 7/2/62 to Japan Air Lines; named *Ayame*. RFS 10/70 and stored at Tokyo.
N5866: S to Boeing 1/4/71 and stored at Wichita, KS. S to Aero American Corp.; D 7/29/71. L to Sunfari Travel Club 1972. S to International Air Leases 4/10/76. Occasionally L to LANICA 1976.
N4339D: S to General Dynamics Corp 10/77; R 11/10/77. Used by GD as an executive aircraft. To IAL Air, Inc. 5/83. L by Rainbow Air 9/83. S to Rainbow Air; RR 1/84. Repossessed by IAL 3/16/84, then re-acquired by Rainbow Air. Parked at Orlando-McCoy 10/84; scrapped there in 1985.   *(L. Callaghan)*

MSN: 62   VN: 22-2-14

N8814E: D 7/14/62 to Delta; IS 7/17/62. Traded in to Boeing; RFS 11/16/73 and handed over at Wichita, KS 12/18/73; TT 35,985.4 hrs.

N900NW: S to Transexecutive Aviation; D 11/8/74 and stored at Marana, AZ. (Apparently N900NW was

not an official registration but appeared on the aircraft).

N8814E: S to American Jet Industries 1/18/79. Ferried to Mojave, CA for storage. Seen there 5/85 with Stirling X-Press titles. S to Charlotte Aerospace 6/85; TT 35,989 hrs. S to Torco Oil Co. 12/93. Extant (bare metal).

(Jon Proctor Collection)

MSN: 63   VN: 22-2-15

N8815E: D 7/2/62 to Delta and IS same day. Traded in to Boeing. RFS 11/16/73 and hand over at Wichita, KS same day; TT 35,893.5 hrs.

N700NW: S to Transexecutive Aviation; D 11/8/74 and stored at Marana, AZ. (Apparently N700NW was not an official registration but appeared on the aircraft). To Monarch Aviation. Converted to cargo configuration; no main deck cargo door.

N8815E: L to Groth Air; D 8/19/77 at Miami, FL. DBR 5/25/78 in takeoff accident at Miami. Scrapped 10/9/81 by BCR Salvage.

(Jon Proctor)

MSN: 64   VN: 22-2-16

N8816E: D 7/11/62 to Delta; IS 7/15/62. Traded in to Boeing; RFS 1/1/74 and handed over at Wichita, KS 1/3/74; TT 35,910.5 hrs. S to Aircraft Investors Retaining Corp. 6/23/75 and stored at Burbank, CA. S to Monarch Aviation 7/8/77. Converted to cargo configuration; main deck cargo door installed.

YV-145C: S to Latin Carga 11/1/79 and handed over at Miami, FL. 11/7/79. Destroyed 11/3/80 in take-off accident at Simon Bolivar Airport, Caracas, Venezuela.   *(Clay Jansson)*

MSN: 65   VN: 22-2-17

N8817E: D 7/19/62 to Delta; IS 7/21/62. Traded in to Boeing; RFS 1/1/74 and handed over at Wichita, KS 1/10/74; TT 35,544.3 hrs. S to Aircraft Investors Retaining Corp. 6/23/75 and stored at Burbank, CA. To Monarch Aviation 6/30/77. Converted to cargo configuration; no main deck cargo door. L to Latin Carga. Destroyed 8/20/77 in accident shortly after takeoff from San Jose, Costa Rica.   *(Delta)*

Convair 990

MSN: 1 VN: 30-5-1

N5601: House airplane. FF 1/24/61 in GD colors; N5601 used for first flight only.

N5601G: RR for balance of certification flight testing.

N711NA: Converted to 990A. L and later S to NASA; D 11/17/64; named *Galileo.* Destroyed 4/12/73 in mid-air collision with U.S. Navy P-3 Orion near Moffett Field, CA. *(General Dynamics)*

MSN: 2 VN: 30-5-2

N5602: FF 3/30/61 in modified GD colors; N5602 used for first flight only.

N5602G: RR for balance of certification flight testing. S to F. B. Ayer & Assoc.; Converted to 990A and D to Garrett AiResearch for refurbishment.

OB-R-765: L and later S to APSA; D 2/1/65.

N990AB: Repossessed 8/73 and stored at Tucson, AZ. S to Gulfstream American Corp.; RR 5/20/80. Moved to Mojave, CA. Turned over to Mojave Airport and now on permanent display at airport. *(Clay Jansson)*

MSN: 3 VN: 30-5-3

N5603: R for first flight only.

N5603G: RR for balance of certification flight testing.

PK-GJA: Converted to 990A and D 1/24/64 to Garuda; named *Pajajaran*. Destroyed 5/28/68 in takeoff accident at Nalla Sopora, India.

(J. Bossenbroek)

MSN: 4　　　　VN: 30-5-4

N5604: R for first flight only. In American Airlines colors with all bare metal areas painted gray.
N5604G: RR for balance of certification flight testing.
PK-GJB: Converted to 990A and D 10/21/63 to Garuda; named *Sriwijaya*.
N7876: RR for transfer to California Airmotive, following lengthy storage at Jakarta. Heavily damaged 9/10/73 in landing accident at Agana, Guam while en route to U.S. Stripped for spare parts and scrapped.　　　　　　　　*(American Airlines)*

MSN: 5　　　　VN: 30-6-1

(Originally a Swissair delivery position.)
N8484H: Under U.S. registration for flight testing. Converted to 990A and S to F.B. Ayer and Assoc. 5/63.
OB-OAG: Refurbished by Garrett AiResearch and L to APSA 11/15/63.
OB-R-728: RR after sale to APSA. Repossessed from APSA summer 1973 and stored at Tucson, AZ.
N990AC: S to General Dynamics 7/76. Moved to Marana, AZ by 1979 and stored. Extant. *(D. Goodwin)*

MSN: 6　　　　VN: 30-6-2

N8485H: Under U.S. registration for flight testing. Originally for SAS; allocated LN-LMA; not taken up.
HB-ICF: D 2/6/64 to Swissair and converted to 990 A at Zürich; named *Schaffhausen*. RFS 10/8/74 and stored at Zürich. Ferried to Hamburg 4/24/75 and scrapped; TT 29,349 hrs.
(Tom Hilldreth)

MSN: 7　　　　VN: 30-6-3

N8497H: Under U.S. reg. for flight testing.
HB-ICA: D 1/12/62 to Swissair; named *Bern*. Converted to 990A at Zürich. L to Air Afrique during 1971. RFS 1/5/75 and stored at Zürich; TT 35,724 hrs.
EC-CNG: S to Spantax 4/19/75; D Zürich-Palma 4/19/75. Damaged in gear up landing at Cologne 4/4/78; repaired and back IS 8/3/78. Last service 4/22/82; RFS and stored at Palma; TT 43,881 hrs., 26,695 landings. Scrapped spring 1991 at Palma.
　　　　　　　　(Terry Waddington)

MSN: 8   VN: 30-6-4

N8498H: Under U.S. registration for flight testing.

SE-DAY: L by Swissair to SAS; D direct from GD 2/23/62; named *Adils Viking.* Sub-L to Thai International during 1962. Converted to 990A at Zürich.

HB-ICG: R to Swissair 2/22/66; named *Winterthur.* Later renamed *Grisons,* then *Graubunden.* RFS 1/10/75 and stored at Zürich; TT 32,759 hrs. **EC-CNF:** S to Spantax 4/5/75; D same day Zürich-Palma. RFS and stored at Palma 12/82; TT 42,166 hrs. Scrapped spring 1991 at Palma. *(General Dynamics)*

MSN: 9   VN: 30-5-5

N5605: D 1/7/62 to American; IS 3/20/62. Converted to 990A at Tulsa; RTS 5/20/63. RFS; TT 12,206 hrs. S to Modern Air 3/13/67. Wet-L to Air France 4/10/67-10/31/67 and flown exclusively between London and Paris. Parked at Chicago-O'Hare 9/1/75.

N8160C: S to Denver Ports-of-Call 7/21/76. RFS 1981 and stored; reg. canceled 2/82. Scrapped at Denver, CO. *(Tom Hilldreth)*

MSN: 10   VN: 30-5-6

N5606: D 1/12/62 to American; IS 3/18/62. Converted to 990A; RTS 4/13/63. RFS; 8,678 hrs.

OD-AEX: S to Lebanese International; D 2/21/66. Destroyed 12/28/68 during Israeli attack at Beirut Airport. *(Peter Keating)*

MSN: 11   V/N: 30-6-5

HB-ICB: D 1/18/62 to Swissair; named *Luzern.* Converted to 990A at Zürich. RFS 12/28/74 and stored at Zürich. Ferried to Hamburg 4/25/75 and scrapped; TT 35,895 hrs.

(Peter Keating)

MSN: 12   VN: 30-6-6

N94280: Under U.S. registration for flight testing.

HB-ICC: D 1/25/62 to Swissair; named *St. Gallen.* Converted to 990A at Zürich. RFS 1/6/75. Donated to Swiss Transport Museum at Lucerne 6/2/75; TT 35,693 hrs. *(B. Badoux)*

(**Note:** *Original msn 12 fuselage and wing roots used as development aircraft for fatigue testing; msn 38 re-numbered msn 12)*

MSN: 13   VN: 30-8-1

PP-VJE: D 3/1/63 to VARIG as 990A.

N987AS: S to Alaska Airlines; 5/67. L to AREA Ecuador (in full colors) 3/68.

N5603: L and later S to Modern Air 10/69. Destroyed 8/8/70 in landing accident at Acapulco. *(Clay Jansson)*

MSN: 14   VN: 30-6-7

(Originally for SAS; allocated SE-DAZ; not taken up.)

HB-ICE: D 8/3/62 to Swissair; named *Canton de Vaud.* Converted to 990A at Zürich. L to Ghana Airways during 1964. RFS after operating Swissair's last actual 990 revenue flight (Tripoli-Zürich) 1/16/75; stored at Zürich; TT 33,894 hrs.

EC-CNJ: S to Spantax; D 6/7/75 Zürich-Palma. Last service 3/10/81; RFS and stored at Palma; TT 41,052 hrs., 25,222 landings. Scrapped spring 1991 at Palma. *(Jon Proctor Collection)*

MSN: 15   VN: 30-6-8

HB-ICD: D 2/3/62 to Swissair; named *Basel-Land.* Converted to 990A at Zürich. L to Ghana Airways during 1964. Destroyed 2/21/70 by sabotage shortly after takeoff from Zürich; TT 24,413.5 hrs. *(Jon Proctor)*

MSN: 16   VN 30-5-7

N5607: D 2/9/62 to American; IS 3/19/62. Converted to 990A at Tulsa; RTS 7/16/63. RFS; TT 12,397 hrs. S to Modern Air 1/4/67.

N5624: RR by Modern Air. L to Nordair during 1968.

N990E: S 8/1/75 to Nomads, Inc. RFS 1981 and stored at Detroit, MI. To Consolidated Components, Inc. (CCI); RR 2/83. To Coronado Aircraft Corp.; RR 3/16/84. Operated by CCI, D/B/A Galaxy Airlines 1985. Stored at Ft. Lauderdale, FL 1986. RR to Christ Is The Answer of El Paso, TX; 3/90. but not operated. Scrapped 4/91 at Ft. Lauderdale.   *(Peter W. Black)*

MSN: 17   VN: 30-6-9

OY-KVA: Registered for first flight only; in SAS colors.

SE-DAZ: L by Swissair to SAS; D direct from GD 4/10/62; named *Ring Viking.* Sub-L to Thai International 5/17/62-12/21/63; named *Srisuriyothai.* Converted to 990A at Zürich.

HB-ICH: R to Swissair 3/27/66. Named *St. Gotthard.* Later renamed *Nidwalden.* L from 3/28/68 to Balair and then sub-L to El Al. L to Air Ceylon in 1968 and again 8/12/74-9/22/74. RFS 11/1/74 and stored at Zürich; TT 33,188 hrs.

EC-CNH: S to Spantax; D 5/31/75 Zürich-Palma. RFS 9/83 and stored at Palma; TT 42,035 hrs. Scrapped 1994 at Palma.   *(Peter Keating)*

MSN: 18   VN: 30-5-8

N5608: D 3/5/62 to American; IS 3/19/62. Converted to 990A at Tulsa; RTS 9/9/63.

OD-AFF: S to MEA; D 6/14/69.

N6844: Traded back to American in exchange for 720B aircraft 2/72.

EC-BZP: S to Spantax; D 4/12/72. RFS 9/84 and stored at Palma; TT 39,428 hrs. Scrapped spring 1991 at Palma.

(Jon Proctor)

MSN: 19   VN: 30-8-2

PP-VJF: D 3/1/63 to VARIG as 990A.
N5625: S to Modern Air 7/1/71. L to Paradise 1000 Travel Club 1972 but not operated.
N8258C: S to Denver Ports-of-Call 6/1/75. RFS 1980 and used for evacuation trainer. Later to city of Denver for fire training at Stapleton Airport; engines removed; in basic POC colors. To be moved from Stapleton to new Denver International Airport; Extant. *(Jon Proctor)*

MSN: 20   VN: 30-8-3

PP-VJG: D 3/1/63 to VARIG as 990A.
N5623: S to Modern Air 6/1/71.
N8259C: S to Denver Ports-Of-Call 6/6/75; RR 6/19/75. RFS and stored; TT 19,833 hrs.; 9,278 landings. Ferried to Marana, AZ for storage. Scrapped 9/86 at Marana.

(Jon Proctor Collection)

MSN: 21   VN: 30-5-9

N5609: D 3/20/62 to American; IS same day. Converted to 990A at Tulsa; RTS 10/11/64. RFS; TT 11,451 hrs. S to Modern Air 1/20/67. L to Nordair during 1968.
EC-BTE: S to Spantax 3/15/70. RFS 10/30/81 and stored at Palma; TT 37,001 hrs. Scrapped spring 1991 at Palma. *(Clay Jansson)*

MSN: 22   VN: 30-5-10

N5610: D 4/4/62 to American; IS 4/9/62. Converted to 990A at Tulsa; RTS 12/14/63. RFS; 11,749 hrs.
EC-BJC: S to Spantax 2/19/67. L to Iberia 4/1/67-12/31/67. Heavily damaged in mid-air collision 3/5/73; RTS 9/73. RFS 11/15/79 and stored at Palma; TT 35,535 hrs. Scrapped spring 1991 at Palma. *(Terry Waddington)*

MSN: 23   VN: 30-5-11

N5611: D 4/4/62 to American; IS 4/12/62. Converted to 990A at Tulsa; RTS 11/22/64. RFS; 12,187 hrs.

EC-BJD: S to Spantax 5/5/67. RFS 4/83 and stored at Palma; TT 38,631 hrs. Scrapped spring 1991 at Palma. *(John Wegg Collection)*

MSN: 24   VN 30-5-12

N5612: D 4/9/62 to American; IS 4/17/62. Converted to 990A at Tulsa; RTS 6/18/63. RFS; TT 10,916 hrs. L to Northeast 1/20/67; named *Flagship Rita*; IS 2/2/67. Returned from lease 4/30/68 and stored.

OB-R-925: L to APSA 6/68.

N6846: Repossessed from APSA 8/16/73 and stored at Marana, AZ. To California Airmotive 9/25/73; R 10/10/73. S to Denver Ports-of-Call 10/23/73.

N8357C: RR 11/26/73. RFS 12/31/84; TT 27,652 hrs., 11,213 landings. Ferried to Marana, AZ for storage. R to Western Continental Holdings 10/87. L to Ciskei International; D via Miami 1/16-17/88. R to Transav, Inc. 9/88. Parked at Ostend, Belgium 5/9/90. S to David Tokoph, Greco Air 9/91 and ferried Ostend-El Paso for storage. Extant. *(Clay Jansson)*

MSN: 25   VN: 30-5-13

N5613: D 5/8/62 to American; IS 5/13/62. Converted to 990A at Tulsa; RTS 11/6/63.

OY-ANI: S to Internord 6/23/67; IS 6/28/67.

N5616: Repossessed by American 10/30/68 and RR.

OD-AFH: S to MEA 6/19/69.

N6845: Traded back to American in exchange for 720B aircraft 3/72.

EC-BZR: S to Spantax 5/8/72. Destroyed 12/3/72 in takeoff accident at Tenerife, Canary Islands. *(B. Lundkvist)*

MSN: 26   VN: 30-5-14

N5614: D 4/21/62 to American; IS 4/22/62. Converted to 990A at Tulsa; RTS 11/23/63.
OD-AFK: S to MEA 12/30/69.
N5614: Traded back to American in exchange for 720B aircraft 1/71. S to Modern Air 1/71. WFU at New York-JFK. Ferried to Miami 11/24/75 and stored. S to Denver Ports-of-Call 4/1/76 (stayed at Opa Locka until at least 8/76). Painted in POC colors but never placed into service; cannibalized for parts and scrapped at Denver late 1978/early 1979.

(Tom Hildreth)

MSN: 27   VN: 30-5-15

N5615: D 5/11/62 to American; IS 5/17/62. Converted to 990A at Tulsa; RTS 12/30/64. S to Modern Air 3/20/68. Named *Polar Byrd I.* L to Nordair during 1868. Parked at New York-JFK 9/1/75.
N8356C: S to Denver Ports-Of-Call 7/20/76. RFS 12/31/84; TT 27,861 hrs., 121,936 landings. Ferried to Marana, AZ for storage. Scrapped 9/86 at Marana.

(Peter W. Black)

MSN: 28   VN: 30-5-16

N5616: D 6/29/62 to American. Destroyed 5/30/63 (prior to 990A conversion) in ground fire at Newark, NJ; TT 1,892 hrs.

(Jon Proctor Collection)

MSN: 29   VN: 30-5-17

N5617: D 5/11/62 to American; IS 6/19/62. Converted to 990A at Tulsa; RTS 8/13/63. S to Modern Air 2/1/68; named *Berliner Bär.*
N713NA: S to NASA 5/18/75 (remained in basic MAT colors through 1976).
N710NA: RR 1978. Stored at Marana, AZ. Reactivated in 1980; stored again 1983.
N810NA: Reactivated in 1988 and converted to Landing Systems Research Aircraft (LSRA) for Space Shuttle landing gear testing; IS April 1993. WFU 8/11/95 and parked at Edwards, CA. Extant.

(Clay Jansson)

MSN: 30   VN 30-5-18

N5618: D 6/5/62 to American; IS 6/9/62. Converted to 990A at Tulsa; RTS 11/1/64.
OD-AFG: S to MEA 6/20/69.
N6843: Traded back to American in exchange for 720B aircraft 10/19/71.
EC-BZO: S to Spantax 1/27/72. Last operational Spantax 990. RFS and stored at Palma. Extant.

operational Spantax 990. RFS and stored at Palma. Extant.   *(K. Ottis)*

MSN: 31   VN: 30-5-19

N5619: D 6/23/62 to American; IS 6/30/62. Converted to 990A at Tulsa; RTS 12/11/64. RFS; TT 7,957 hrs.
OD-AEW: S to Lebanese International 10/19/65. L to Balkan Bulgarian 6/68-12/68. Destroyed 12/28/68 during Israeli attack at Beirut Airport.

(J. Bossenbroek)

MSN: 32   VN: 30-5-20

N5620: D 2/21/63 to American as 990A; IS 3/3/63.
EC-BNM: S to Spantax 1/29/68. Destroyed 1/5/70 shortly after takeoff from Arlanda, Stockholm, Sweden.

(J. Bossenbroek)

MSN: 33   VN: 30-5-21

N5601: D 1/18/63 to American as 990A; IS 1/29/63.
OD-AFJ: S to MEA 9/19/69.
N5601: Traded back to American in exchange for 720B aircraft 12/16/70. S to Modern Air 12/19/70. WFU 10/74 and stored at Opa Locka, FL. S to Denver Ports-of-Call 8/25/76. Painted in POC colors but never placed into service. Cannibalized for spare parts. Fuselage and wings purchased in 1980 by Thomas Pierce and William Carley; moved to Tri-County Airport, Erie, CO. Restaurant closed in 1991. Extant.   *(William T. Larkins)*

MSN: 34 VN: 30-5-22

N5602: D 1/31/63 to American as 990A; IS 2/7/63.
SE-DDK: S to Internord 12/2/67.
N5606: Repossessed by American 10/30/68.
EC-BQQ: S to Spantax 4/18/69. RFS 6/86 and stored at Palma; TT 36,185 hrs. Scrapped 1994 at Palma, although fuselage (minus wings) remains intact, on landing gear.

(Terry Waddington)

MSN: 35 VN: 30-5-23

N5603: D 2/8/63 to American as 990A; IS 2/18/63.
OD-AFI: S to MEA 7/11/69.
N5603: Traded back to American in exchange for 720B aircraft 3/71.
EC-BXI: S to Spantax; D 4/10/71. L briefly to Iberia. RFS 6/29/81 and stored at Palma; TT 35,481 hrs., 20,599 landings. Scrapped spring 1991 at Palma.

(Peter Keating)

MSN: 36 VN: 30-5-24

N5604: D 3/21/63 to American as 990A; IS 4/1/63.
OY-ANL: S to Internord 3/16/68.
N5612: Repossessed by American 10/30/68.
EC-BQA: S to Spantax 1/17/69. L to Iberia 3/69-3/70. RFS 12/85 and stored at Palma; TT 38,093 hrs. Scrapped at Palma 1994.

(Jon Proctor Collection)

MSN: 37 VN: 30-5-25

PK-GJC: D 9/3/63 to Garuda as 990A; named *Majapakit.*
N7878: To California Airmotive 6/73; refurbished and S to NASA.
N712NA: RR; named *Galileo II.* Destroyed 7/17/85 during aborted takeoff at March AFB, CA. *(J. Gear via Don Linn Collection)*

MSN: 38 -- See MSN 12

Appendix I
Aircraft Operators

CONVAIR 880

COMPANY NAME	START-UP DATE	ACFT. OPERATED (MSN)
Aerovías Quisqueyana	1978*	52
Air Malta	1976*	44, 54
Air Trine	February 1976*	57
Airtrust Singapore (Orient Pacific Airways)	Summer 1975*	21, 44, 47, 54
Air Viking	August 1973*	48
Alaska Airlines, Inc.	August 30, 1961	54
Bahamas World	June 1976*	07, 60
Cathay Pacific Airways Ltd.	April 8, 1962	See Story
Central American Airways	February 1980*	46
Civil Air Transport	July 12, 1961	44
Compass	1975*	57
Concordia Corp.	1976*	21
Delta Air Lines, Inc.	May 15, 1960	See Story
Fair Air/F&B Livestock	Dec. 20, 1976	51
Falair, Inc.	1971*	46
Federal Aviation Administration (FAA)	August 1961*	55
Flying Fish Company (Potter Aircraft Co.)	July 1981*	18
Florida Travel Club	1977*	60
Four Winds, Inc.	January 1981*	56
Freelandia Travel Club	1973*	57
General Dynamics Corp.	1977*	61
Groth Air Services	August 1977*	07, 63
Gulf Air	1976*	44
Haiti Air Freight	May 1985*	17
Indy Air Travel Club	1977*	56, 60
Holiday Magic OY	August 1973*	46
Inair Panamá	February 1979*	41, 52
Japan Air Lines Co. Ltd	October 1, 1961	See Story
Jetaway	1976*	43
Jonian Airways	1972*	46
KLM Royal Dutch Airlines	July 1, 1963	37, 53, 56
Latincarga	February 1979*	64
Lineas Aéreas de Nicaragua S.A.	July 14, 1972	See Story
Monarch Aviation	1977*	41, 46, 50, 52, 63, 64, 65
Northeast Airlines, Inc.	Dec. 15, 1960	See Story
Onyx Aviation, Inc.	May 1978*	17, 56
Elvis Presley	April 1975*	38
Profit by Air, Inc. (Profit Express)	Fall 1981*	04, 46
Rainbow Air	September 1983*	61

Rowan Drilling Co./RDC Marine, Inc.	January 1975*	48
Seagreen Air Transport	January 1982*	17
Sentinel Jets, Ltd.	March 1979*	58
SERCA Costa Rica	November 1984*	50
Sunfari Travel Club	1972*	61
Sunjet International, Ltd.	(operated as Four Winds)	
Swissair	September 1961	43, 45
Trans World Airlines, Inc.	January 12, 1961	See Story
Travel-A-Go-Go	1976*	43
Glenn W. Turner	August 1971*	48
United States Navy	Summer 1981*	55, 56
Venezolana Internactional De Aviación, S.A. - (VIASA)	October 1961	37, 53, 56

CONVAIR 990

Aerolíneas Peruanas, S.A. (APSA)	Dec. 1, 1963	02, 05, 24
Air Afrique	1971	07
Air Ceylon	1968, 1974	17
Air France	April 10, 1967	09
Alaska Airlines, Inc.	Summer 1967	13
American Airlines, Inc.	March 18, 1962	See Story
AREA Ecuador	3/68	13
Balair	1968	17
Balkan Burgarian Airlines	6/68*	31
Ciskei Int'l	1988	24
Christ Is The Answer	(Not operated)	16
Denver Ports-Of-Call	1974*	See Story
El Al	1968	17
Galaxy Airlines	1984*	16
Garuda Indonesian Airways	September 1963*	03, 04, 37
Ghana Airways Corporation	1964	14, 15
Iberia	1967*	22, 35, 36
Internord	June 28, 1967	25, 34, 36
Lebanase International Airways	Dec. 23, 1965	10, 31
Middle East Airlines Airliban	July 1969*	See Story
Modern Air Transport	January 1967*	See Story
National Aeronautics & Space Admin.	November 1964*	01, 29, 37
Nomads, Inc.	August 1975*	16
Nordair	1968*	16, 21, 27
Northeast Airlines, Inc.	February 2, 1967	24
Scandinavian Airlines System	May 18, 1962	08, 17
Spantax, S.A.	1967	See Story
Swissair	March 9, 1962	See Story
Thai International Airways	May 18, 1962*	08, 17
Viação Aérea Rio-Grandense, S.A. (VARIG)	March 1963*	13, 19, 20

*- *Exact dates not confirmed.*

Note: *It has not been possible to confirm that operations actually took place under all of the names listed. In some cases a carrier may have taken possession of the aircraft but never operated it. In other instances company names may be duplicates of the same service.*

Appendix II
CONVAIR 880 REGISTRATION INDEX

Reg.   **Msn**

Nicaragua:

Reg.	Msn
AN-BIA	39
AN-BIB	09
AN-BLW	04
AN-BLX	36

Taiwan:

Reg.	Msn
B-1008	44M

Switzerland:

Reg.	Msn
HB-ICL	43M
HB-ICM	45M

Haiti:

Reg.	Msn
HH-SMA	17

Panama:

Reg.	Msn
HP-821	41
HP-876	52

Japan:

Reg.	Msn
JA8021	57M
JA8022	58M
JA8023	59M
JA8024	60M
JA8025	61M
JA8026	46M
JA8027	48M
JA8028	49M
JA8030	45M

Iceland:

Reg.	Msn
TF-AVB	48M

Hong Kong:

Reg.	Msn
VR-HFS	47M
VR-HFT	43M
VR-HFX	37M
VR-HFY	54M
VR-HFZ	53M
VR-HGA	44M
VR-HGC	56M
VR-HGF	58M
VR-HGG	60M

Venezuela:

Reg.	Msn
YV-145C	64
YV-C-VIA	53M
YV-C-VIB	56M
YV-C-VIC	37M

United States:

Reg.	Msn
N1RN	57M
N42	55M
N112	55M
N375	32
N4339D	61M
N48058	43M
N48059	44M
N48060	47M
N48062	54M
N48063	56M
N54CP	46M
N55NW	07
N5858	46M
N5863	48M
N5865	57M
N5866	61M
N59RD	48M
N700NW	63
N88CH	58M
N800NW	17
N801AJ	03
N801TW	1/42
N802AJ	06
N802TW	02
N803AJ	08
N803TW	03
N804AJ	10
N804TW	05
N805TW	06
N806AJ	12
N806TW	08
N807AJ	13
N807TW	09
N808AJ	15
N808TW	10
N809AJ	19
N809TW	12

Reg.	Msn
N810AJ	20
N810TW	13
N811AJ	22
N811TW	14
N812AJ	23
N812TW	15
N813AJ	24
N813TW	18
N814AJ	32
N814TW	19
N815AJ	35
N815TW	20
N816AJ	40
N816TW	22
N817AJ	04
N817TW	23
N818AJ	09
N818TW	24
N819AJ	36
N819TW	25
N820AJ	39
N820TW	26
N821TW	27
N822TW	28
N823TW	30
N824TW	31
N825TW	32
N826TW	33
N827TW	34
N828TW	35
N829TW	39
N830TW	40
N871TW	01
N8477H	54M
N8478H	05
N8479H	08
N8480H	12
N8481H	20
N8482H	22
N8483H	23
N8486H	44M
N8487H	37M
N8488H	56M
N8489H	01M
N8490H	53M

Reg.	Msn
N8491H	46M
N8492H	09
N8493H	18
N8494II	34
N8495H	39
N84790	55M
N880AJ	01
N880EP	38
N880JT	60M
N880NW	11
N880SR	07
N880WA	51
N8801E	04
N8802E	07
N8803E	11
N8804E	16
N8805E	17
N8806E	21
N8807E	29
N8808E	36
N8809E	38
N8810E	41
N8811E	50
N8812E	51
N8813E	52
N8814E	62
N8815E	63
N8816E	64
N8817E	65
N900NW	62
N90450	36
N90452	09
N90455	39
N94284	43M
N94285	45M

U.S. Navy:

Reg.	Msn
161572	55M

Note: *For ease in identification, M follows the msn if an 880 was built as an "M" model, although it is not considered part of the serial number.*

Appendix III
CONVAIR 990 REGISTRATION INDEX

Reg.	Msn

Spain:

EC-BJC	22
EC-BJD	23
EC-BNM	32
EC-BQA	36
EC-BQQ	34
EC-BTE	21
EC-BXI	35
EC-BZO	30
EC-BZP	18
EC-BZR	25
EC-CNF	08
EC-CNG	07
EC-CNH	17
EC-CNJ	14

Switzerland:

HB-ICA	07
HB-ICB	11
HB-ICC	12
HB-ICD	15
HB-ICE	14
HB-ICF	06
HB-ICG	08
HB-ICH	17

Thailand:

HS-TGE	17

Norway:

LN-LMA	06

Peru:

OB-OAG	05
OB-R-728	05
OB-R-765	02
OB-R-925	24

Lebanon:

OD-AEW	31
OD-AEX	10
OD-AFF	18
OD-AFG	30
OD-AFH	25
OD-AFI	35
OD-AFJ	33
OD-AFK	26

Sweden:

OY-ANI	25
OY-ANL	36
OY-KVA	17

Indonesia:

PK-GJA	03
PK-GJB	04
PK-GJC	37

Brazil:

PP-VJE	13
PP-VJF	19
PP-VJG	20

Denmark:

SE-DAY	08
SE-DAZ	14/17
SE-DDK	34

United States:

N5601	01/33
N5601G	01
N5602	02/34
N5602G	02
N5603	03/13/35
N5603G	03
N5604	04/36
N5604G	04
N5605	09
N5606	10/34
N5607	16
N5608	18
N5609	21
N5610	22
N5611	23
N5612	24/36
N5613	25
N5614	26
N5615	27
N5616	25/28
N5617	29
N5618	30
N5619	31
N5620	32
N5623	20
N5624	16
N5625	19
N6843	30

N6844	18
N6845	25
N6846	24
N710NA	29
N711NA	01
N712NA	37
N713NA	29
N7876	04
N7878	37
N810NA	29
N8160C	09
N8258C	19
N8259C	20
N8356C	27
N8357C	24
N8484H	05
N8485H	06
N8497H	07
N8498H	08
N94280	12
N987AS	13
N990AB	02
N990AC	05
N990E	16

SELECTED BIBLIOGRAPHY

BOOKS

Davies, R.E.G. *Airlines of Latin America Since 1919.* Washington D.C.: Smithsonian Inst. Press, 1984.

—. *Airlines of the United States Since 1914.* London: Putnam, 1972.

Eastwood, A.B & Roach, J.R. *Jet Airliners Production List.* Middlesex: The Aviation Hobby Shop, 1992.

Franklin, Roger. The Defender — *The Story of General Dynamics.* New York: Harper & Row, 1986.

Killion, Gary L. *The Convair Twins — 240 to 640.* London: Macdonald and Jane's, 1979.

Rummell, Robert W. *Howard Hughes and TWA.* Washington D.C.: Smithsonian Inst. Press, 1991.

Serling, Robert J. *Eagle — The Story of American Airlines.* New York: St. Martin's/Marek, 1985.

—. *Howard Hughes' Airline.* New York: St. Martin's/Marek, 1983.

Wegg, John. *General Dynamics Aircraft and their Predecessors.* London: Putnam, 1990.

Young, Gavin. *Beyond Eden Rock — The Story of Cathay Pacific Airways.* London: Brookmount House, 1988.

PERIODICALS (listed by date)

"GE Engines Going Commercial," *American Aviation,* July 5, 1954, p19.

"Turboprop Convairs Are Coming," *American Aviation,* Nov. 22, 1954, p32-34.

"Convair Dart Airliner Details Revealed," *Aviation Week,* Aug. 1, 1955, p79-81.

"Convair Jet Has Transcontinental Potential," *Aviation Week,* April 9, 1956, p99.

"How Convair Rates Its Medium-Range Jet," *American Aviation,* April 9, 1956, p70-72.

"Decisions of '55 Shaped Equipment Pattern," *American Aviation,* April 23, 1956, p29-31.

"Convair Bids for Medium Range Jet Market," *Aviation Age,* May 1956.

"Hughes' Jet Plan Rekindles Old Debate," *Aviation Week,* May 21, 1956, p41.

"Hughes Seeks CAB Permission To Build New Jet Transport," *American Aviation,* May 21, 1956, p20.

"Order for Ten Convair Golden Arrow Jet Airliners Announced," *Delta Digest,* June-July 1956, p10.

"Boeing Weighs Short Range Jet Transport," *Aviation Week,* June 11, 1956.

"TWA, Delta Order Convair Skylark 600," *Aviation Week,* June 18, 1956, p40-41.

"GE Bids for Big Share of Civil Jet Sales," *American Aviation,* Aug. 13, 1956, p33-34.

"Convair 880 Details Show Flexibility," *Aviation Week,* Oct. 15, 1956, p57-58.

"Calif. Eastern May Purchase Convair 880 for Overseas Routes," *Aviation Week,* Oct. 29, 1956, p42.

"Convair Test Program Increases 880 Speed," *Aviation Week,* March 18, 1957, p33.

"The Convair 880," *The Aeroplane,* April 26, 1957, p588-590.

"Low Lead Time, Lightness Mark J79," *Aviation Week,* May 27, 1957, p29-30.

"Heavy Skin, Fail-Safe Features Mark 880," *Aviation Week,* June 17, 1957, p82-85.

"Boeing Plans Short-Range Jet Designed for 130 Passengers," *Aviation Week,* July 22, 1957, p48.

"New Area Rule Concepts May Give Jet Airliners 50 Mph. Speed Gain," *Aviation Week,* Aug. 12, 1957, p29.

"Area Rule May Boost Jet Transports' Speed; NACA," *American Aviation,* Aug. 26, 1957, p47-48.

"United Wants 880," *Aviation Week,* Oct. 7, 1957.

"Convair To Offer J57-Powered 880," *American Aviation,* Nov. 18, 1957, p30.

"New Period of Uncertainty Faces TWA," *Aviation Week,* Jan. 6, 1958.

"Capital Puts 880 Near Breakeven Point," *Aviation Week,* Feb. 3, 1958.

"Convair Proposes Military Uses for 880," *Aviation Week,* Feb. 17, 1958.

"880's Cabin Comes in Three Versions," *American Aviation,* May 19, 1958.

"Industry Studies Transport Area Rule," *Aviation Week,* July 14, 1958, p49-52.

"Producing the Convair 880," *The Aeroplane,* Aug. 1, 1958, p172-175.

"American Orders Area-Ruled Jetliners," *Aviation Week,* Aug. 4, 1958, p38-39.

"Area Rule Concept Fits Convair's 600 to Meet Jet Age Problems," *Aviation Week,* Sep. 8, 1958, p50-52.

"Convair 600 Structure Parallels 880's," *Aviation Week,* Sep. 15, 1958.

"Convair's Model 600," *The Aeroplane,* Oct. 3, 1958, p517-519.

"Convair 880/600," *Interavia,* No. 11/1958, p1195-1199.

"Convair Rolls Out Its First Model 880," *Aviation Week,* Dec. 22, 1958, p34-35.

"Convair's 880 and 600," by Charles Meredith, *Flying,* Jan. 1959, p. 47, 83.

"The Problem of Howard Hughes," by C.J.V. Murphy and T. A. Wise, *Fortune,* Jan. 1959, p79.

"Hughes Tool: A Gusher of Money," *Fortune,* Jan. 1959, p82-83,171-175.

"Jet Bugaboos No Problem For 880," *The San Diego Union,* Feb. 1, 1959, pC1.

"Swing-Tail Convair 600 Proposed," *Aviation Week,* Feb. 23, 1959.

"American Sets Transport Disposal Pace," by Glenn Garrison, *Aviation Week,* April 27, 1959, p42.

"A Deadline for Howard Hughes?", *Fortune,* June 1959, p.112-113/226-233.

"Engines Testing Out on Convair 880," by Fred Hunter, *Airlift,* July 1959, p49.

"Continental May Buy Four Convair 600s," *Aviation Week,* Aug. 3, 1959.

"Keeping Up With This Amazing Jet Age...," *Newsweek,* Jan. 11, 1960, p72-74.

"Convair's 880 is Ready to Go...Fast," by William J. Coughlin, *Airlift,* Feb. 1960, p.22-25.

"An Airline's Dream," *Delta Digest,* Feb. 1960, p4-7.

"Delta 880 Training Paves Way for May 15 Service," by R. Sweeney, *Aviation Week,* May 2, 1960, P74.

"CAB Approves Hughes-TWA Pact, Permitting 707, 880 Purchases," *Aviation Week,* July 11, 1960.

"General Dynamics Writes Off Jet Cost,"*Aviation Week,* Oct. 3, 1960.

"Northeast Awaits Release of 880," by David H. Hoffman, *Aviation Week,* Nov. 7, 1960.

"Hughes Releases Six 880s to Northeast," *Aviation Week,* Nov. 28, 1960, p39.

"Convair Rolls Out First Model 990 Jet; Testing Begins," *Aviation Week,* Dec. 5, 1960, p42-45.

"TWA Seeks Early 880 Deliveries; Financing Program Nears Closing," *Aviation Week,* Dec. 19, 1960, p41.

"Paperwork Delays TWA 880 Introduction," by David H. Hoffman, *Aviation Week,* Jan. 2, 1960, p33.

"Hughes-TWA Dispute Status of Trustee," *Aviation Week & Space Technology,* Jan. 29, 1961, p41-44.

"Convair 990 Modifications Delay FAA Certification for 6 Months," *Aviation Week,* Mar. 27, 1961, p38.

"Takeoff Distance Cut on Convair 880-M," by William S. Reed, *Aviation Week,* May 29, 1961, p48-50.

"Pace Predicts Additional Losses from Convair 990 Development," *Aviation Week,* May 8, 1961, p45.

"Hughes Financing Delay Fails," *Aviation Week,* June 5, 1961, p43.

"Convair 990," by Donald P. Germeraad, *Flying,* Sep. 1961, p24-28.

"How a Great Corporation Got Out of Control, Part I" by Richard A. Smith, *Fortune,* Jan. 1962, p64.

"Hughes Tool Cancels Order for 13 Convair 990s; Keeps 4 880s," *Los Angeles Times,* Jan. 17, 1962.

"How a Great Corporation Got Out of Control, Part II," by Richard A. Smith, *Fortune,* Feb. 1962, p20.

"990 Demonstrates Safety and Economy," by William S. Reed, *Aviation Week & Space Technology (AW&ST),* Feb. 26, 1962, p69.

"How Interim 880s Saved Swissair," *Airlift,* Feb. 1962, p22-25.

"General Dynamics Jet Write-offs Boost 1961 Loss to $143 Million," *AW&ST,* April 2, 1962, p29.

"The Convair 880," *Flying Review International,* Nov, 1966, p212-213.

"Convair 990," by Günter G. Endres, *Aircraft Illustrated,* March 1976, p.128-132.

"The Convair 880," by Jon Proctor, *Journal of the American Aviation Historical Society,* Fall 1976, p202.

"The Convair 990," by Jon Proctor, *Journal of the American Aviation Historical Society,* Wtr. 1976, p274.

"Convair 880 in S.E.Asia," by Leon C. Callaghan, *Air Pictorial,* April 1982, p148-150.

"The Incomparable Coronado," by Jon Proctor, *Airliners,* Summer 1988, p26-35.

"The Passing of the Convair 990," by G.C. Kehmeier, *Wings West Magazine,* 4th qtr. 1991

"Convair's Skylark: The Eight-Eighty," by Jon Proctor, Airliners, Sep./Oct. 1995; p22

Acknowledgements

I would like to thank American Aviation Historical Society members Martin Cole and William T. Larkins, who encouraged and assisted with my original Convair jets research projects over 20 years ago. Ray Wagner, archivist at the San Diego Aerospace Museum provided hospitality and assistance during my visit to the Convair archives, now located at that facility.

Photographic support and, in many cases, research assistance, was generously provided by the following companies: General Dynamics, Alaska Airlines, American Airlines, Cathay Pacific, Delta Air Lines, Japan Air Lines, NASA, Swissair, TWA, and the United States Navy.

I was given access to the private photo collections of many friends, including Tom Brown, Leon Callaghan, Nigel Chalcraft, Barney Deatrick, Bruce Drum, Tony Eastwood, Phil Glatt, Donnie Head, Tom Hildreth, Curtis Hunslander, Dick Hurley, Clay Jansson, Peter Keating, Tsunehiro Kouda, Don Levine, Don Linn, Tom Livesey, Jay Miller, William T. Morgan, Robert S. Morris, Harry Peat, Larry Ivan Potoski, Larry Pullen, Marion Pyles, Alex Reinhard, Jay Selman, Bob Shane, Jay Sherlock, Mark Stevens, John Stewart, Ron Suttell, Arnold Swanberg, Jim "Jet" Thompson, Georg Von der Mühll, Terry Waddington and John Whitehead.

Valuable research assistance and, in some cases, photographs were provided by Hiroshi Ando, Tim Averett, Hal Bagnall, Ed Betts, Morten S. Beyer, Peter Black, Michael Bolden, Phil Brooks, C. Buckley, Steve Bush, Jeff Cacy, Steve Caisse, Dan Colburn, William B. Carmody, George Cearley, Mark S. Daniels, Elwood David, Ed Davies, R.E.G. Davies, J.W. Duff, Thor Eklund, Simon Ellwood, Chris English, George Farinãs, Robert Farrugia, Paul Goldschaag, Clint Groves, Peter Gysel, Scott Haskin, Carlos Herrera, Gene Hooker, Gary Jackson, Gary L. Killion, Chad Koppie, Bob Kopitzke, William T. Larkins, Herbert C. Lineberger, Rich Lytle, Mike Machat, Martin Marlow, Ray Mattox, Dan McIntyre, Duncan Mills, Wally Moran, C. Robert Muller, Warren Munkasy, Guy Norris, Harriette Parker, Edward Peck, G. Pennick, V.J. Pieroni, Mike Potter, Bill Proctor, Bob Proctor, Milo Raub, Manual Rezende, Tony Ristuccia, Jack N. Robertson, Robert W. Rummel, Antonio Sanson, Robert J. Serling, Michael Shapira, Tom Sheridan, Jim Shotwell, Harry Sievers, Daniel Sproat, Derek Trusk, C.J. Turner, Ben Valley, John Wegg, Harold B. Whitman, Archibald P. "Speed" Wilson, Nigel Winfield, James P. Woolsey, and Giulio Zambon.

With a multitude of contributors to remember, I probably have omitted one or more names. To those left out, my sincere apologies.

I would also like to thank Delta Air Lines Director of Corporate Communications Steven Forsyth, for permission to reprint the Paul Bennett story from *Delta Digest*.

Finally, special gratitude is expressed to: Captain Carlos Herrera, who provided an exceptional amount of information and names of others who plugged many holes in my research; *Airliners* magazine Managing Editor Nicholas A. Veronico; Billie Jean Plaster, copy editor; Fred Chan, copy editor and a constant source of support; Keith Armes and Bruce & Pauline Drum, who made this book possible.

Jon Proctor
P. O. Box 968
Sandpoint, Idaho 83864

February 1996